# A Southern Collection

MORRIS
MUSEUM of ART

# A Southern Collection

BY ESTILL CURTIS PENNINGTON
Curator of Southern Painting

MCMXCII

MORRIS COMMUNICATIONS CORPORATION
AUGUSTA, GEORGIA

Select works from a permanent collection
of painting in the South prepared for the
opening of the Morris Museum of Art,
September 24,1992.

*With a foreword*
*by William S. Morris, III*
*Chairman of the Board of Trustees*

MORRIS
MUSEUM of ART

Library of Congress Cataloging-in-Publication Data

Pennington, Estill Curtis.
    A Southern Collection / by Estill Curtis Pennington.
        p.   cm.
    Includes index.
    ISBN 0-9618270-5-X (hardcover)          ISBN 0-9618270-6-8 (softcover)
    1. Painting, American – Southern States – Exhibitions.
    2. Morris Museum of Art (Augusta, Ga.) – Exhibitions.  I Title.
    ND220.P47   1992
    759.15'074'75864–dc20                                          92-23560
                                                                        CIP

# Contents

Foreword   6
*William S Morris, III*

Note on Catalog Organization
   and Acknowledgements   9

Regard for Southern Art Since 1960   11
*Estill Curtis Pennington*

Antebellum Portraiture   20

Art of the Civil War   32

The Black Presence in Southern Painting   44

Southern Still-Life Art   56

Landscape Painting in the South   68

Southern Impressionism   94

Works on Paper   122

Twentieth-Century Art   144

The Self-Taught Southern Artist   178

Contemporary Southern Painting   210

Checklist of the Permanent Southern Collection   237

Index   245

# *Foreword*

For six generations, Augusta, Georgia, has been home to the Morris family. Our roots are deep in the Southern soil. Art – in many forms – has long been a part of the Morris family endeavors.

It is fitting, therefore, that two important concepts, family ties and artistic heritage, come together in the Morris Museum of Art.

It has been my longtime dream to establish an art museum in memory of my parents, William Shivers Morris, Jr. and Florence Hill Morris. I can never repay them for the start they gave me in life, the inspiration they imparted to me, and the legacy they left me. I hope this museum will stand as a continuing tribute to their memory and to their love for this community and its people.

In this, the Morris Museum of Art's inaugural exhibition, which presents a survey of unique and remarkable works from our Southern collection, we hope to illuminate and celebrate an artistic heritage as rich and diverse as the South itself.

So much of our journey through life is made wonderful by the works of God and our ability to see them. One of God's richest blessings is to allow us to see and enjoy his creation. It is God, the original Artist, who painted the rainbow, the sunrise, the sunset, and the morning mist in such a way as to capture our attention and wonder. It is not unusual then that man would try to imitate the works of our Creator.

And so each generation produces its painters, sculptors, and artisans who bring fresh, new imagination to what God created and painted long, long ago.

It is my hope that the Morris Museum of Art in time will play a major role in the cultural life of our community, our region, and our nation, that it will become a focal point for the creative energy of Southern art scholarship, and that by preserving and building upon our artistic heritage we will create a legacy to enrich the lives of generations to come.

The opening of the Morris Museum of Art is a tribute to the efforts of many people: to my family, who have shared the dream, and who will continue to be trustees of the vision; to

GEORGE INNESS, JR.
1853-1926

*Rainbow in Georgia*
Oil on canvas, 16 x 24 inches
1989.01.087

many friends and trusted advisers, who have given support and encouragement; and to the late Dr. Robert Powell Coggins, whose personal quest to discover the art and artists of the South gave us the foundation on which to build a unique and significant collection.

It is a tribute, especially, to Estill Curtis Pennington, Southern art historian, whose dedication and scholarship have given the institution both shape and substance; to the Morris Museum of Art's first director, Keith Claussen, a true friend, who has shared my vision and enthusiasm for this undertaking; and, finally, to my wife, Sissie, whose interest in and eye for things of beauty have always been an inspiration to me.

WILLIAM S. MORRIS, III

September 24, 1992

WILLIAM THOMPSON RUSSELL SMITH
1812-1896

*Mount Vernon*
Oil on canvas, 1836-1876, 17¼ x 23¼ inches
1989.01.191

From the outset, the purpose of this catalog has been to feature select masterworks from the permanent collection in a format offering the kind of detailed biographical, formal, and curatorial information necessary to provide a foundation for further study of both the artist and the object.

In each instance, all pertinent literature has been cited with one exception: The more familiar biographical dictionaries have been omitted.

Nor has space permitted the repetition of the entire itinerary of the "Art and Artists of the South" exhibition in each entry for objects from that show. That itinerary is reproduced at the end of this note.

The catalog itself is organized into sections that correspond exactly with the actual flow of the gallery spaces within the museum. These categories are meant to be neither definitive nor restrictive. Rather, they are intended to provide a pathway of exploration for critical and historical purposes.

By and large they are chronological, moving in a steady progression from the early nineteenth century to the present day. Some have a stronger thematic function – for instance, the section on the black presence – while others, like the landscape and works-on-paper categories, are capacious repositories.

The brief remarks that divide the individual sections are little more than sound-bites from the cultural audio-visual library. Each of the categories deserves a much greater in-depth look than can be achieved at this time, especially by one individual. But again, to extend the metaphor, they are meant to be roadsigns on the same pathway toward understanding. Read them accordingly and look to the possibility of further explication as the profound goal of this institution.

This catalog was made possible by the collections and assistance of many institutions and individuals. In particular, I am grateful to the New Orleans Museum of Art for materials on the Woodwards; to the extensive holdings of the Historic New Orleans Collection for materials on Louisiana artists; to the Archives of American Art for rare primary materials on Eliot Clark; to the Fine Arts Library of the Smithsonian; and to the

*Art and Artists of the South:*
*The Robert P. Coggins Collection*

### EXHIBITION SCHEDULE

Cheekwood Fine Arts Center, Nashville, Tennessee,
June 9-October 14, 1984.

San Antonio Museum Association, Museum of Art,
San Antonio, Texas, November 11-December 30, 1984.

Hunter Museum, Chattanooga, Tennessee, January 13-
March 3, 1985.

Huntsville Museum, Huntsville, Alabama, March 24-
June 16, 1985.

The Museum of the Confederacy, Richmond, Virginia,
July 1-September 1, 1985.

Telfair Academy of Arts and Sciences, Savannah,
Georgia, September 17-November 2, 1985.

Columbia Museum of Art, Columbia, South Carolina,
January 5-March 30, 1986.

Mint Museum, Charlotte, North Carolina, April 13-
June 15, 1986.

High Museum of Art, Atlanta, July 25-August 31, 1986.

Mississippi Museum of Art, Jackson, September 12-
November 9, 1986.

The Arkansas Art Center, Little Rock, November 20-
January 11, 1987.

holdings of the Roger Houston Ogden Collection in New Orleans. Historical work acquired from the gallery of Robert M. Hicklin, Jr. in Spartanburg, South Carolina, came with impeccable curatorial files, often recording the entire bibliographic and curatorial life of an object, as did contemporary works from the Arthur Roger Gallery of New York and New Orleans.

I should also like to express my appreciation for the generous help of these colleagues: Judy Throm, Cecilia Chinn, Jim Sauls, Kim Tuck, Garnett McCoy, Liza Kirwin, Eric Widing, Franklin Reilman, Ellen Miles, Robert G. Stewart, Ken Barnes, Roger Ogden, John Bullard, Dode Platou, Rob Hicklin, and Arthur Roger. At Morris Communications, I should like to thank Lydia Inglett for the very beautiful job of design and production, and Jeff Barnes for laboriously photographing each work. Thanks also to Andra Conley Eanes for meticulous copy-editing, to David Kaminsky for superb color separations, and to Genia L. Weinberg for graphic production assistance.

My deepest thanks and sincere devotion to Mr. and Mrs. William S. Morris, III for the courage and vision to undertake a project of such breathtaking proportion. It is my fervent prayer that the visionary institution they have erected on the levee by the Savannah River will live long and prosper.

My own efforts on this catalog are dedicated to my two partners in this project, Louise Keith Claussen and Robert John Kuhar. As museum director and editor, Keith has guided this project with discipline and a thoroughness to detail that has often defied reason. As an architect, Bob has effectively dealt with the limits of the space even as he has consistently provided graceful proportion and empathic response to the art itself. In this process, both have become my dear friends, for which I am truly grateful.

– E.C.P

More than thirty years ago, on the eve of the centennial of the Civil War, the Corcoran Gallery of Art mounted an exhibition titled "American Painters of the South."

Herman Warner Williams, Jr., director of the Corcoran at that time, had more than a passing interest in the art of the South, for as a gifted historian of Civil War illustrations, he had been intellectually involved with the region for several years.

The exhibition that opened there on New York Avenue in Washington, D.C., April 23, 1960, was far from modest, even by current blockbuster standards. One hundred twenty-four objects were on display, covering the time span from tidewater colonialism to the siege of Sumter. Accompanied by a modestly sized, but highly informative catalog of some forty pages, "American Painters of the South" would remain the definitive source on the topic for the next twenty-five years, until "Painting in the South" opened at the Virginia Museum in 1985.

Several themes in the Corcoran catalog echo down the antiquarian halls of time with far more than the reverberating noise of simple truth, simply expressed. Eleanor Quandt, the chief curator of the show, begins with an honest statement of need: "A history of painting in the American South has yet to be written." She proceeds to explain that Southern art was known, up to that time, only to a few "local antiquaries."

Nor had surveys of extant material culture been conducted in the South. Under such circumstances, with limited available evidence from which to draw proper conclusions on the subject, it is not surprising that she should feel "the average museum visitor may be acquainted with only half a dozen names of painters in the South, and may have a very lopsided view of the history of American art as a result." Even now, forty years later, despite the considerable efforts of two generations of curators and collectors since that time, Quandt's lamentable conclusion remains largely unchallenged.

From the outset, the Corcoran show set particular boundaries that remain highly valuable for the student of painting in the South. The geographic range extended along the Mason-Dixon line from Maryland to Missouri, precisely the border drawn by Congress throughout the antebellum period to define the South in socio-economic terms. The upper South, or border states of Maryland, Kentucky, and Missouri, had strong Southern characteristics of place as well as folk ways that remain intact. The obvious deep South regions of Louisiana and the Carolinas speak for themselves. Not only does the catalog introduction define the geographic locale of Southern art, but the thematic association as well. While recognizing that "many leading painters in the area, although American-born, were Southerners neither by birth nor permanent residence," Quandt goes on to justify their inclusion: "Their pictures, however, became part of the cultural milieu of the South and inevitably influenced indigenous developments."

This distinction between indigenous art and external influence establishes the critical dialectic of Southern art studies.

Since art is never created in a vacuum, we must search for source, interaction, and artistic response to prevailing trends. In this way, as Quandt has noted, we may more fully understand the significance of art "as a record of the social scene and the tastes of the time."

Many of the artists represented had long been a part of the larger canon of American art, especially the portraitists. Charles Bridges, John Wollaston, the Peale family, Thomas Sully, Chester Harding, and William Edward West had appeared in many standard histories, albeit for their Northern activities. Still others, like Jacob Eichholtz, Cephas Thompson, and Henry Benbridge, were only slightly less known.

Inclusion of George Caleb Bingham was of singular importance. He was a native of the South who painted lively scenes of Southern commerce, as well as insightful historical fantasies of the Southern political process. To eliminate him from the canon of Southern art would have been to have robbed the South of one of its most perceptive and innovative geniuses, regardless of his personal politics and feelings on secession and slavery.

Other artists emerged from this exhibition as worthy of future consideration, including the desperately ambitious portraitist George Cooke, with his dreams of a Southern national gallery of art, and Richard Clague, the atmospheric landscape painter of Louisiana who practiced an American form of the French Barbizon style twenty years before the New York tonalists. While he was a better-known artist, Richard Caton Woodville's headliner genre pictures began to attract a wider interest after their appearance in Washington.

More than twenty-five years would pass before the subject of painting in the South was again explored on an expansive scholarly level. During that time the study of American art was

Christopher Murphy, Jr.

beginning to emerge from the confines of antiquarian interests and modernist approbation. Most of the proponents of modernism tended to view all American art as one steady movement toward "the triumph of American painting" represented by abstract expressionism.

As a response to such notions of singleness of purpose, many scholars of American culture sought to affirm consensus rather than acknowledge multi-cultural complexity and diversity. Instead of seeking an understanding of American art that evoked the formal values apparent in each work, art historians like Oliver Larkin and Joshua Taylor produced volumes that presented American art as an illustration of that much-heralded objective correlative, "American character."

Larkin published *Art and Life in America* in 1949 to great acclaim, winning the Pulitzer Prize for history that year. From the outset, his consensus mentality was apparent. His stated goal was "to show how these arts have expressed American ways of living and how they have been related to the development of American ideas, particularly the idea of democracy."

With that agenda in hand Larkin proceeded to create a linear, causal pathway for American art, manipulated toward a unilateral purpose and seen through a thinly disguised pair of antiquarian spectacles, polished up with the cloth of presentism. Unlike an erudite formalist, who might let the art and life of the past express themselves in their own terms, Larkin quotes and illustrates in a manner to support his own quest for the democratic spirit.

Except for passing nods toward the more familiar Southern architectural achievements, especially in the Greek Revival era, he does not examine Southern art at all. Considering the momentum created by prize-winning surveys within the American academic community, this fact may explain subsequent failure to include the South in survey works.

Still, during this first period of interest in American art, many landmark exhibitions were held that did expand the horizons of the field. Several American institutions, notably the Metropolitan Museum of Art, the Detroit Institute of Art, and the National Collection of Fine Art, began to organize shows that presented American painting in the fullness of serious scholarly study.

While the Metropolitan's exhibits and all-important American Wing established a focal point in the field, it was really the endeavors of Edgar P. Richardson and Dr. Joshua Taylor which propelled American art studies onto their present course. In 1954 Richardson founded the Archives of American Art at the Detroit Institute. After its move to the Smithsonian in 1970 this collection of primary documents became the ultimate source in the field.

At the same time, Taylor began to focus the efforts and energies of the National Collection of Fine Arts upon American art studies, culminating in that institution's transformation into the National Museum of American Art.

Neither Taylor nor Richardson pursued the topic of Southern art. During Richardson's tenure, and the subsequent tenure of William E. Woolfenden, the Archives conducted no original field work in the South and gathered no Southern documents beyond those that happened to reside in existing northeastern collections. While the Archives expanded energetically into the Midwest, and on to California, the South was ignored. Finally in the late '70s a tentative fledgling effort was put forth in Texas with local funding. At the same time, work was begun in the field in Georgia and Kentucky.

Much of Taylor's work culminated in the landmark exhibition "America as Art," organized as part of the national bicentennial celebrations of 1976. The energies that the bicentennial sparked have been beneficial for American art studies. If the market is any indicator, the great increase in prices for American art during the past sixteen years signifies the final arrival of our native talent, old and new. Maybe.

Taylor's lengthy catalog for "America as Art" poses vital questions. Like all students of our culture, he begins with an attempt to identify the ways in which we reflect shared Western values even as we veer off into our own individual expression. Ultimately, Taylor's exploration of American art is motivated by a search for specific American contributions to "artistic concepts of directions in art…." Toward that end he admits that his method is "a very narrow way of looking at American art."

Again, while Taylor re-examines the profound landscape art of this country, and the latent strains of realism and naturalism in the art of social relations, there is no reference to the art of the South. Yet again, American art is defined by the activities of the artistic community in the narrow corridor from Boston to New York to Philadelphia, with a passing nod to Washington as the font of public patronage. While certain forms of Southern art may follow the same international trends in style Taylor detects in the American canon, the larger study of Southern culture is excluded from his consensus mentality. Classic American culture as envisioned by the consensus historian is monolithic, possessed of the resources to obtain great wealth from the bounty of a virgin wilderness, and relentlessly surging toward collective enlightenment and prosperity.

Southern culture, even at this point, is hierarchical, and

ELLA SOPHONISBA HERGESHEIMER
1873-1943

*Vase of Flowers, Drapery, Inkwell*
Oil on canvas, 21¾ x 25½
1989.01.075

consumed with the divisions of that hierarchy, particularly as they relate to the ongoing resonance of the past in the present. Southern culture is also vividly oral, and this propensity may have inspired a strong narrative tradition in painting. Inter-relationships in Southern life and culture ensure apposition to larger American life. The South is always tempered by change but has not been, to this point, swept away and reinvented every generation, as is the case with American popular culture.

Of course, the single greatest dynamic in Southern life has been race. The South has been forced, by dramatic and tragic circumstances, to confront directly that most subliminal of American issues and has profited greatly as a result. To this day, the image of the African-American in Southern life and letters remains the most compelling semiotic element, demanding far deeper, and, indeed, far more honest interpretation and presentation than we have seen.

While perhaps not self-consciously aware of these needs and issues, it was in this climate of taste that the Virginia Museum of Art convened a group of diverse Southern curators and art historians in Richmond in 1979 to discuss the launching of an investigative effort that would culminate in the exhibition, "Painting in the South: 1564-1980." In her introduction to the exhibition catalog, Ella-Prince Knox notes that even "twenty years after the Corcoran's pioneering effort" a definitive history of painting in the South had yet to be written.

With this task in mind, Knox defined the goals of the exhibition's curators: "In order to document and clarify the art of the South, the curators have chosen to take a broad view, both geographically and chronologically. Their purpose has been to bring to light an image of the South free from the misinterpretations that often shroud and obscure it. With its themes at once divergent and distinct, the South has long had trouble looking at and interpreting itself; definitions of it come hard. For this reason, the curators did not attempt to set forth a definitive statement of what exactly is Southern about the painting of the South, nor did they apply the label 'Southern' only to those artists who have lived exclusively within the region."

Even at the relatively short span of seven years from the time "Painting in the South" opened, it seems that these generous terms and challenging extensions should still form the boundaries of study in the field. Most subtle of all is the idea of "painting in the South," as opposed to Southern painting or Southern painters. This definition suggests activity within an environment, rather than activity circumscribed by passports or birthrights.

What the Virginia effort addressed was the need for a far

more thorough body of material to regard than had previously been seen. Mining that material was more than an antiquarian effort and, at least in the beginning, less than an exercise in connoisseurship. Functioning as cultural anthropologists, we must first discover, as did, indeed, the generations of antiquarians who came before, who painted what and where and when. With that body of knowledge in place, we can proceed with those canons of formal critical analysis that constitute the ultimate regard with which we may view the achievements of the artists at hand.

As a catalog, *Painting in the South* represents the first serious application of American art-historical methodology to the Southern arts. Curators of each predetermined historical epoch brought to the catalog the considerable achievements of their individual disciplines. The chronological divisions, though broad, were appropriate, and in some cases innovative.

Carolyn Weekley of Colonial Williamsburg pursued the colonial period, extended past the revolution to 1790. This was an important precedent, suggesting the lingering aspects of style in Southern painting that, to my eye, characterize it to the present day. Linda Simmons of the Corcoran took on the brief, but intensely active, period from 1790 to 1830. In parallel fashion, the spirit of the South in this time was still in sync with a variety of national trends. Most historians agree that the rise of Southern nationalism occurred in the aftermath of the Missouri Compromise and the Jacksonian presidency.

By simultaneously restricting and extending the Old South period, from 1830-1900, Jessie Poesch confirmed an intriguing notion that the Civil War occurred in the midst of a surging cultural wave. To see the South as an entity leading up to, and beyond, that war is to take a far larger picture than the usual rise-and-fall-of-the-Old-South historiography affords. Finally, Patrick Stewart and Donald Kuspit divided this century exactly in half. Stewart's essay on the period from 1900 to 1950 is strongest in recognizing corollary trends in the literature of the South. Needless to say, as that time frame is the age of Faulkner, Glasgow, the Fugitives, and a host of other Southern grand masters, such correlation could hardly be avoided.

At precisely the same moment "Painting in the South" was underway, Dr. Robert Powell Coggins of Marietta, Georgia, had commissioned Dr. Bruce Chambers to write a catalog for an exhibition organized from his vast collection of Southern art. "Art and Artists of the South: The Robert Powell Coggins Collection" opened in June 1984 and traveled through the South for more than two years. While the Virginia show achieved a survey of extant materials primarily discovered in existing public holdings, "Art and Artists of the South"

represented a deliberate effort to assemble a private collection on the subject. Dr. Coggins' assembled works of art were proof of the most profound and broad-ranging efforts to date. Within the Coggins Collection, lesser works by great masters vied for public attention with major works by unknown artists. Well-received and well-attended, "Art and Artists of the South" was a landmark event, a watershed by which subsequent efforts may be measured.

In 1989, William S. Morris, III of Augusta, Georgia, purchased the Coggins Collection with the intention of creating a museum devoted to exhibitions and continued research. As such, it is the first museum of its type in the South.

With the Coggins holdings as a foundation, further supplemented by a large deposit of works from the Coggins estate, the Morris Museum of Art has the largest survey collection on the topic in existence. This foundation has been further expanded by numerous, judicious acquisitions, notably in the new, vital area of the Southern self-taughts. Because Dr. Coggins did not collect mid-twentieth-century art or contemporary art with the fervor he collected the arts of the past, these areas had to be addressed extensively.

As the Morris Museum of Art opens, the challenges to the study of painting in the South are no less intense than previously.

William Gerdts, in the introduction to his section on the South in his monumental *Art Across America*, can still note that the "art of the South has, until recently, been terra incognita." Gerdts confirms the outsider position of Southern painting by acknowledging that "Southern painting has not been incorporated into the larger framework of American art history, and works by southern artists rarely appear in broader surveys."

With the opening of the Morris Museum of Art, there is now both an opportunity and a setting for serious study of Southern painting. Because the museum will always have a broad historical survey of works on display, the general public should find the exercise both stimulating and enjoyable. At the same time, demanding Southern cultural issues can be assimilated, and proper correlations of the type Larkin and Taylor envisioned can be pursued. It will be interesting to see what themes, if any, emerge. Already I have the notion that much of Southern art is characterized by a tendency that gives greater metaphoric significance to prevailing international stylistic trends when practiced in the South.

Impressionism, for example, was a radical movement that transformed composition in painting from evocations of light into light itself. In the South, impressionism takes on far deeper symbolic meaning as a means of capturing the nostalgic mood of times and places that may never have existed except in more vivid imaginations.

Lest it be thought that the Morris Museum of Art will be entirely captivated by the distant past, it should be stated from the outset that the greatest interpretative challenges to painting in the South have occurred within the past fifty years. Modern Southern art is rarely abstract, giving evidence very early on of those strains of magic realism and extended narration that one finds in contemporary New Orleans and Atlanta.

In our own time, the eccentric genius of the self-taught Southern artist, often black and from a rural setting, creates an intellectual dilemma of provocative proportion. Within this dilemma, older Southern concerns of racism collide with extremely strong contemporary longings to find and promote original genius, untainted by the relentless harangues of the mass media.

To rise to the occasion and meet those challenges, the Morris Museum of Art will pursue an active and energetic exhibition policy based on the permanent collection and augmented by carefully selected loans. In this way, those interested in the history and progress of painting in the South can expand a vocabulary of form that is currently far too narrow to be truly articulate. This expansion is the very nature of art history.

In his landmark book, *The Anxious Object*, Harold Rosenberg begins his discourse on the interrelationship between modern abstract art and art history with an exciting definition of terms. Having stated that "tradition was an inescapable ingredient of the art of earlier centuries, proposing both what to paint and how to paint it," he goes on to define the role of art history: "Art history decides what art is. In turn, art decides what shall move us as beauty." To be moved by the art of the South, the art historian and eager viewer must embark upon a voyage of discovery that not only defines what art is, but where it is to be found. Having done that, the culture of the South, not to mention the nation, should prove richer for affirming the diversity and energy that always seem to characterize the American experience long after consensus on our manners has failed to detect the palpable beatings of our hearts.

ESTILL CURTIS PENNINGTON
Curator of Southern Painting

Drawings by Christopher Murphy, Jr., 1902-1973
Robert Powell Coggins Art Trust, Morris Museum of Art

# Antebellum Portraiture

During those days before the Civil War, in the time now called the Old South, itinerant portrait artists of varying abilities traveled throughout the countryside taking likenesses of eager sitters. Some of these artists were native Southerners whose skills reflected mainstreams of national and international style. Still others were visiting painters from the north, whom the art historian Anna Wells Rutledge has called "birds of passage."

For a frontier people living in the era before photography, portraiture had an obvious appeal. Preserving the likeness of a family member, or recording some particularly important event, such as marriage, the birth of a child, or a death, was integral to the ritual of life. Portraits served two functions: They were decorative objects, perhaps the only works of art in the house, and they became important icons for owners and descendants. Passed from generation to generation, portraits provided continuity and a locus for the veneration of family customs.

Many of the itinerant artists repeated certain anatomical and stylistic conventions, which has led to the creation of an entire body of largely mythic notions concerning portrait substance and significance. In truth, artists did not go about the South with canvases pre-painted with headless bodies, upon which to place the heads of susceptible sitters.

Antebellum portraiture accounts for one of the largest artistic categories in the Southern canon, and offers a wealth of material for continued study in the field.

## JOHN WESLEY JARVIS

1780-1840

Born in England; apprenticed to Edward Savage in Philadelphia, c. 1793; active as an itinerant portraitist in the South, 1810-1834, especially in New Orleans, 1821-1834; died, New York City.

### *Mrs. William Palfrey*

c. 1821
Oil on canvas, 30 x 25½ inches
Robert Powell Coggins Art Trust,
Morris Museum of Art COG-0195

#### PROVENANCE
From the family, in passing; to Felix Kuntz, New Orleans; to Sloan Auction House, Washington D.C., sale 701, lot 1351; by purchase to Robert Powell Coggins Collection; to Robert Powell Coggins Art Trust, Morris Museum of Art.

#### LITERATURE
Audubon, John James. *Journal of John James Audubon Made During His Trip to New Orleans in 1820-1821.* Boston, 1929.

Dickson, Harold Edward. *John Wesley Jarvis, American Painter, 1780-1840.* New York City, 1949.

Dunlap, William. *A History of the Rise and Progress of the Arts of Design in the United States of America.* New York City, 1869.

Mahe, John A., II and Rosanne McCaffrey. *Encyclopedia of New Orleans Artists 1718-1918.* Historic New Orleans Collection, New Orleans, 1987.

Quick, Michael. *American Portraiture in the Grand Manner: 1720-1920.* Los Angeles, 1981.

#### ARCHIVAL SOURCES
Archives of American Art, Smithsonian Institution.

Historic New Orleans Collection.

New York Historical Society.

Jarvis was one of the Northern itinerants who found a period of portrait activity in the deep South to be both lucrative and amusing. He bragged to Dunlap that on his first trip to New Orleans, "My purse and pockets were empty. I spent 3000 dollars in six months, and brought 3000 to New York. The next winter I did the same." While undoubtedly he was successful, his braggadocio did not amuse Audubon, who encountered him there in January 1821. Struggling to establish himself as an artist, Audubon "walked to Jarvis the Painter and shewed him some … Drawings," as a means of appealing to Jarvis for work as an assistant "to finish his portraits i.e. the Clothing and Ground." Jarvis dismissed him, directing him to return the next day when he asked Audubon so many questions that the naturalist "thought that he feared my assistance." They parted without speaking again, Audubon feeling, "No doubt he looked on me as I did on him as an Original, and a Craked Man."

However preposterous Jarvis may have been, he was an accomplished artist in the fledgling American romantic style. *Mrs. Palfrey* is warmly colored and presents a calm, benign visage toward posterity. The Palfrey family were Boston merchants who moved to the Louisiana territory in the late eighteenth century. Colonel William, postmaster general of the Continental army, was lost at sea in 1780. His widow, the subject of this portrait, moved with her son, John Palfrey, to Louisiana in 1804. Jarvis painted her grandson, Henry William Palfrey of New Orleans, who, ironically, also was lost at sea, in 1866.

## TREVOR THOMAS FOWLER

1800-1871

Born, Dublin, Ireland; studied at the Royal Academy, London, 1829, and at the Royal Hibernian Academy, Dublin, 1830; active as an itinerant in Kentucky, Mississippi, and Louisiana, along the river route, and in New Orleans, 1829-1871; died, New Orleans.

### *Mrs. James F. Robinson (Willina S. Herndon)*

1851, signed and dated, edge of table
Oil on canvas, 36 x 29 inches
1989.04.250

While Fowler apparently began an international itinerancy in the deep South prior to 1840, his first major public notices came for portraits of William Henry Harrison and Henry Clay, rivals in the presidential election of 1840, which were exhibited in New Orleans that same year. Between 1840 and 1854, Fowler was one of the more energetic and highly visible seasonal itinerants working between New Orleans and Louisville, Kentucky. On several trips he worked in tandem with the Louisiana artist Theodore Sidney Moise. Moise was a rather accomplished provincial animalier who rendered the pets that often appeared in the duo's more ambitious genre portraits.

During a trip to Kentucky in 1851, Fowler painted Mrs. Robinson, wife of the governor, and, hence, First Lady of Kentucky. Several signature Fowler conventions appear in this work: a warm, slightly flushed coloration, a delicate line defining anatomical contouring and modeling, offset by the rather graceful flowing scarf and still-life detail.

#### PROVENANCE
From the family, in passing; to William Barrow Floyd, Lexington, Kentucky; by purchase to Southeastern Newspapers Corporation; by gift to Morris Museum of Art.

#### LITERATURE
Bruns, Mrs. Thomas Carter Nelson, comp. *Louisiana Portraits*. National Society of the Colonial Dames of America in the State of Louisiana. New Orleans, 1975.

Mahe, John A., II and Rosanne McCaffrey. *Encyclopedia of New Orleans Artists 1718-1918*. Historic New Orleans Collection, New Orleans, 1987.

New York Historical Society. *Catalog of American Portraits in the New York Historical Society*. New Haven, Connecticut, 1974.

Pennington, Estill Curtis. Notes on the Artists, in *Mississippi Portraiture*. National Society of the Colonial Dames of America in the State of Mississippi. Laurel, Mississippi, 1987.

Whitley, Edna Talbott. *Kentucky Ante-Bellum Portraiture*. National Society of the Colonial Dames of America in the Commonwealth of Kentucky. Louisville, Kentucky, 1956.

#### ARCHIVAL SOURCES
Historic New Orleans Collection.

Works Progress Administration, Lives, New Orleans Artists, New Orleans Museum of Art.

## WILLIAM HARRISON SCARBOROUGH

1812-1871

Born, Dover, Tennessee; studied with John Grimes in Nashville, Tennessee and with Horace Harding in Cincinnati; active in North and South Carolina as well as in Georgia from his studio base in Columbia, South Carolina, 1846-1871; died, Columbia.

### *Portrait of a Young Girl and Older Man*

c. 1855, signed on stretcher
Oil on canvas, 49¾ x 39½ inches
1989.01.173

Scarborough's work has many of the characteristics of romantic Southern portraiture: a warm coloration, a seemingly tactile quality in background and costume detail, and a close proximity of the figure to the picture plane. While the subjects in this work are unknown, Scarborough, like Sully, did keep an account book that may lead to their identity. The scale of this work is very much in keeping with high-style Southern taste in the ten years prior to the outbreak of the Civil War, when stately houses with large formal rooms were often dominated by grand manner portraits that might be called "Plantation Baroque."

**PROVENANCE**
Acquired from a home in Columbia, South Carolina, by Ray Holsclaw, Charleston, South Carolina; by purchase to Robert Powell Coggins Collection; by purchase to Southeastern Newspapers Corporation; by gift to Morris Museum of Art.

**LITERATURE**
Hennig, Helen K. *William Harrison Scarborough, Portraitist and Miniaturist.* Columbia, South Carolina, 1937.

National Society of the Colonial Dames of America in the State of Georgia. *Early Georgia Portraits.* Athens, Georgia, 1975.

Swenssen, Lise. *South Carolina Art: Selections from the South Carolina State Museum Collection.* Columbia, South Carolina, 1991.

**ARCHIVAL SOURCES**
South Carolina State Museum, Columbia.

**EXHIBITION HISTORY**
"'Art and Artists of the South' and Recent Acquisitions," Georgia Museum of Art, University of Georgia, Athens, January 9-February 21, 1988.

## NICOLA MARSCHALL

### 1829-1917

Born, St. Wendell, Rhenish Prussia; as a young man received some training at the Dusseldorf, Germany, Academy; active in New Orleans and Mobile, Alabama, 1849-1851, in Marion, Alabama, 1851-57, 1859-61, and in Louisville, Kentucky, 1873-1917; died, Louisville.

### *Young Girl with Cat*

c. 1859, signed middle right
Oil on canvas, 28½ x 36 inches
Robert Powell Coggins Art Trust,
Morris Museum of Art COG-9450

While Marschall is reputed to have had at least some formal training in Europe prior to his arrival in America in 1849, it was of a very rudimentary nature. In 1857 he returned to Europe where, according to his great-grandson's account, he studied in Munich and in Italy. The portrait at hand almost certainly indicates his further training, and the mature style in which he worked until his death. Actually, this work is more of a genre painting than a traditional portrait. Close examination of the symbolic elements indicates a little girl not at all pleased with the sitting. The fixed stare, disheveled clothing, and lost shoe are elements of a well-constructed disarray. The young girl clinging somewhat desperately to the poor cat in her grasp has a certain look of disdain for the viewer, who cannot help but notice the careful attention to detail in the still life, and the Empire stool that serves as a very solid prop.

**PROVENANCE**
From the family, in passing; to Mrs. Ada R. Leapley, Wichita, Kansas; to Mrs. Ona Drake, Wichita; to Robert Snyder, Russell, Kansas; by purchase to Robert Powell Coggins Collection; to Robert Powell Coggins Art Trust, Morris Museum of Art.

**LITERATURE**
Alabama State Department of History and Archives. *Nicola Marschall, Designer of the First Confederate Flag.* Montgomery, 1931.

Costlow, Owsley C. *The Life of Nicola Marschall.* Unpublished manuscript prepared by Marschall's great-grandson with the assistance of the artist's personal scrapbooks, still in the possession of the family in Louisville, Kentucky. (A copy may be found in the Center for the Study of Southern Painting, Morris Museum of Art.)

National Society of the Colonial Dames of America in the State of Alabama. *Alabama Portraits Prior to 1870.* Mobile, Alabama, 1969.

Sauls, James, in Chambers, Bruce. *Art and Artists of the South.* Columbia, South Carolina, 1984.

Whitley, Edna Talbott. *Kentucky Ante-Bellum Portraiture.* National Society of the Colonial Dames of America in the Commonwealth of Kentucky. Louisville, Kentucky, 1956.

**ARCHIVAL SOURCES**
Center for the Study of Southern Painting, Morris Museum of Art.

Filson Club, Louisville, Kentucky.

National Museum of American Art, Smithsonian Institution.

## WILLIAM CHARLES ANTHONY FRERICHS

1829-1905

*Lizzie Neigh Wier*

1864, signed and dated lower right
Oil on ticking, 54 x 42 inches
Robert Powell Coggins Art Trust,
Morris Museum of Art COG-XX11

Born in Ghent; educated at the Royal Academy in The Hague, Netherlands; active in the area of Greensboro, North Carolina, 1855-1865; died, Tottenville, New Jersey.

Oral history surrounding this painting suggests that the subject was the daughter of the president of Greensboro Female College in North Carolina where Frerichs lived and taught from 1854 until 1863. A disastrous fire and the upheaval of the Civil War interrupted his career there, launching him on an itinerant flight from federal forces and institutional demise that persisted until he left the South in 1865.

Stylistically, this portrait marks an interesting departure for Frerichs. In the midst of war and chaos, he has painted an idyllic image of a young girl in a very colorful, indeed, highly keyed, palette reminiscent of certain northern European Biedermier works. While totally unlike his landscape paintings, it is also the only surviving portrait from his Southern period.

PROVENANCE
From the Wier family in passing; discovered by Howard Smith, Madison, North Carolina; to Robert M. Hicklin, Jr., Inc., Spartanburg, South Carolina; to Robert Powell Coggins Collection; to Robert Powell Coggins Art Trust, Morris Museum of Art.

LITERATURE
Chambers, Bruce. *Art and Artists of the South.* Columbia, South Carolina, 1984.

Kelly, James C. *The South on Paper.* Spartanburg, South Carolina, 1985.

Safford, Hildegarde J. and Benjamin F. Williams. *W.C.A. Frerichs.* Raleigh, North Carolina, 1974.

# Art of the Civil War

The outbreak of hostilities between the federal government and the Confederate States of America coincided with the rise of the illustrated "penny press." These sometimes sentimental, sometimes sensational newspapers rose to the occasion by commissioning the first published depictions of fierce battles and noble leaders.

Artists of note worked on both sides. The landscape painter Joseph Rusling Meeker and the marine and genre artist Winslow Homer both began their careers as interpreters of the Civil War scene. Alfred Waud managed to represent both sides. On the Southern side, William Aiken Walker, Conrad Wise Chapman, and Nicola Marschall all were pressed into service.

As Bruce Chambers has pointed out in *Art and Artists of the South*, the war inspired a veritable cottage industry of historical art and illustration for more than 30 years. Several artists in this collection were among those who, in Chambers' view, "provided information to a public whose curiosity about the war had remained unabated through Reconstruction and the early years of the New South. The endless stream of memoirs, historical reappraisals and fiction by the war's participants created a lively market for military illustrators until the time of the Spanish-American War's new heroes [as though] the great war had never ended and its great battles continued to be refought. ..."

## EDWIN AUSTIN FORBES

1839-1895

### Defending a Battery - Confederate Cavalry Charge

c. 1863, initials lower right
Pen and ink on paper, 10¾ x 14⅞ inches
1989.01.053

### Writing it Up - Heroic Soldier of the Pen

c. 1863
Pen and ink on paper, 4⅞ x 7¼ inches
1989.01.054

Born, New York City; studied with Arthur Fitzwilliam Tait in New York; active in the Virginia theater of operations during the Civil War, 1862-1864; died in New York.

Forbes was one of the most successful artist-correspondents covering the Civil War for the line-cut tabloids that sprang up to meet the need of an eager public hungry for news from the front. While artists like Eastman Johnson and Winslow Homer returned to civilian careers, Forbes continued as the definitive artist of the front, with a series of publications issued from 1876 to 1889. As Bruce Chambers has written, the "artist-correspondents of the war, for North and South alike, faced most of the same hazards as the troops with the added obligation of producing – against deadlines – timely and articulate images of the war that would not only inform and even entertain the folks back home, but also rally their support to the cause."

**PROVENANCE**
Thomas Moebs Americana and Fine Books; to Jack Tittleman, Olympia Galleries, Ltd., Philadelphia and Atlanta; by purchase to Robert Powell Coggins Collection; by purchase to Southeastern Newspapers Corporation; by gift to Morris Museum of Art.

**LITERATURE**
Chambers, Bruce. *Art and Artists of the South*. Columbia, South Carolina, 1984.
    . *Art and Artists of the Civil War*. Unpublished manuscript in production with Smithsonian Institution Press.
Dawson, William Forrest. *Civil War Artist at the Front: Edwin Forbes' Life Studies of the Great Army*. New York, 1957.
Forbes, Edwin Austin. *Thirty Years After: An Artist's Story of the Great War*. New York, 1890.
Moebs, Thomas. List #72, 182 Original Civil War Drawings by Edwin Forbes. Atlanta. (Undated ephemera. One copy may be found in the Center for the Study of Southern Painting, Morris Museum of Art.)

**ARCHIVAL SOURCES**
Edwin Austin Forbes Collection, Library of Congress.

**EXHIBITION HISTORY**
"Art and Artists of the South: The Robert Powell Coggins Collection," 1984-86. (See note on catalog organization for complete exhibition schedule.)

## JOHN A. MOONEY

c. 1843-1918

*Surprise Attack Near Harper's Ferry*

c. 1868
Oil on canvas, 54⅛ x 96¼ inches
1989.01.120

Birthplace unknown; active in Virginia (?) 1863-1898 (?), and in Washington, D.C., 1898-1902; died, Richmond.

Elusive details about Mooney's life only add to the tragic pathos of his sad existence. Like Conrad Wise Chapman he served through some of the bloodiest campaigns of the war, emerging shell-shocked and desolate. *Surprise Attack …* is really a memory painting composed in the years after the war, for which several preparatory sketches survive. Ambitiously composed, it depicts a horrifying episode set in an otherwise idyllic scene. The looks of shock and anguish upon the fleeing soldiers' faces compound the ironic sense of surprise interrupting an undoubtedly pleasant moment of relaxation. Indeed, the entire history of the war is punctuated with just such sad episodes: fleeting moments of peace violently terminated by bloody assault.

To this eye, Mooney compounds that ironic sense of vulnerability by his very choice of subject matter. Traditionally, the male nude, posed in an idyllic landscape, provides a vehicle for transcendental reflections upon the natural state of man. Here, that state is at once violated and enhanced by the juxtaposition of figures and setting.

**PROVENANCE**
Westmoreland Club, Richmond, Virginia, to Young's Art Shop, Richmond, to Gallery Mayo, Richmond; to James Williams, Savannah, Georgia; by purchase to Robert Powell Coggins Collection; by purchase to Southeastern Newspapers Corporation; by gift to Morris Museum of Art.

**LITERATURE**
Chambers, Bruce. *Art and Artists of the South.* Columbia, South Carolina, 1984.

**ARCHIVAL SOURCES**
The Valentine Museum, artist's files, Richmond, Virginia.

**EXHIBITION HISTORY**
"Art and Artists of the South, The Robert Powell Coggins Collection," 1984-86. (See note on the catalog organization for complete exhibition schedule.)

# "MONOGRAMMIST M"

## The Lost Cause

1869, inscribed lower right
Oil on canvas, 19¾ x 26¹³⁄₁₆ inches
1989.01.004

The original source for this "Lost Cause" image was a painting by the Cincinnati-based artist Henry Mosler, which was exhibited at the National Academy of Design in 1868. That work was pendant to a work called *Leaving for War*, which shows the same Southern highlander departing in high spirits and with a cavalier backward glance at the humble homestead he leaves behind. Here, his return is not a happy one. Having lost the war, he faces peace with diminished resources, his home in ruins, his family dispersed – a symbolic representation of the South itself.

As Chambers points out, the work also affirms the importance of the Southern yeoman to Confederate war efforts. Clearly, all Confederate soldiers and officers were not drawn from the mythic legions of genteel planters. Generals Lee and Jackson themselves reflect the varied nature of Southerners in uniform. Like the buckskin-clad regular at hand, Jackson was a highland man. Such men proved to be the backbone of Lee's army, those whom an observer at the time could call " … the dirtiest men I ever saw, a ragged, lean and hungry set of wolves. Yet there was a dash about them that the Northern men lacked."

**PROVENANCE**
From Sammy J. Hardeman, Atlanta; to Robert Powell Coggins Collection; by purchase to Southeastern Newspapers Corporation; by gift to Morris Museum of Art.

**LITERATURE**
Chambers, Bruce. *Art and Artists of the South.* Columbia, South Carolina, 1984.

Neely, Mark E., Harold Holzer and Gabor S. Bobbitt. *The Confederate Image.* Chapel Hill, North Carolina, 1987.

**EXHIBITION HISTORY**
"Art and Artists of the South: The Robert Powell Coggins Collection," 1984-86. (See note on catalog organization for complete exhibition schedule.)

## XANTHUS R. SMITH

1839-1929

Born in Philadelphia; studied with his father, the artist Russell Smith, and at the Pennsylvania Academy of Fine Arts, 1855-58; active in the Charleston theater of war, 1862-1864.

### *Battle of Kearsarge & Alabama 1892*

1892, signed and dated lower right
Watercolor on paper, 19¾ x 29¾ inches
1989.01.193

Although not on the scene when the famous engagement between the Kearsarge and the Alabama took place, Smith began to paint images of the event as early as 1868, reconstructing details from contemporary accounts. In 1876 he exhibited a monumental painting based on the subject at the Philadelphia Centennial Exposition. This work was acquired for the Union Club of Philadelphia where it still hangs. The Alabama met the Kearsarge off the coast of Cherbourg, France, on June 19, 1864. Superior Union naval experience put a quick end to one of the Confederacy's few top-line vessels.

**PROVENANCE**
As per label, verso: "Close of the engagement between the U.S. Steamship Kearsarge and Confederate Cruiser Alabama Off Cherbourg France, June 19th, 1864. Painted for M.D. Evans, Esq. by Xanthus Smith"; Evans Collection, in passing; to David Ramus Gallery, Atlanta; by purchase to Robert Powell Coggins Collection; by purchase to Southeastern Newspapers Corporation; by gift to Morris Museum of Art.

**LITERATURE**
Chambers, Bruce. *Art and Artists of the South.* Columbia, South Carolina, 1984.

Ferrante, Anne. "Early Photographic Images of the Smiths: A Family of Artists." *Archives of American Art Journal.* Smithsonian Institution.

Smith, Xanthus. *An Unvarnished Tale.* Unpublished autobiographical manuscript, Smith Family Papers, Archives of American Art, Smithsonian Institution.

Vose Galleries. *The First Exhibition in Fifty Years of Oil Paintings by Russell Smith (1812-1896), and His Son Xanthus Smith (1839-1929).* Boston, 1977.

**ARCHIVAL SOURCES**
Archives of American Art, Smithsonian Institution.

**EXHIBITION HISTORY**
"Art and Artists of the South: The Robert Powell Coggins Collection," 1984-1986. (See note on catalog organization for complete exhibition schedule.)

# WILLIAM GILBERT GAUL

1855-1919

## *The Infantryman*

c. 1905, signed lower left
Watercolor on board, 16½ x 10 inches
1989.01.062

Born, Jersey City, New Jersey; studied with John George Brown at the National Academy of Design, New York; active in the South at Van Buren, Tennessee, near Nashville, 1881-1911; died, Ridgefield, New Jersey.

While Gaul was not an artist-correspondent working on the front during the war, he established a career as an illustrator of military scenes for popular magazines. He was a history painter in the European military tradition of artists like the French painter Meissonier, to whom Lathrop favorably compares him, citing an ability to "seize a character in many of its bearings at once. …" The illustrative work at hand has that cavalier quality of repose in the face of danger that the Southern audience of the late nineteenth century had come to expect in depictions of Confederate forces. Gaul's illustrations of military episodes have a highly dramatic visual appeal, as may be seen in the remarkable series of prints, *With the Confederate Colors*, issued by the Southern Art Publishing Company in 1907. However, he also produced several finely developed landscape works in a late Barbizon style, drawn from life on a farm in rural Tennessee.

**PROVENANCE**
Greg Javo, Atlanta; by purchase to Robert Powell Coggins Collection; by purchase to Southeastern Newspapers Corporation; by gift to Morris Museum of Art.

**LITERATURE**
Chambers, Bruce. *Art and Artists of the South*. Columbia, South Carolina, 1984.

Davis, Louise. "Turnips and Triumphs in Tennessee: A Portrait of the Artist Gilbert Gaul." *Tennessean* magazine, (August 18-September 1, 1974).

Kelly, James C. "Landscape and Genre Painting in Tennessee, 1810-1985." *Tennessee Historical Quarterly* 44, no. 2 (Summer 1985).

Lathrop, George Parsons. "An American Military Artist." *The Quarterly Illustrator* 1, no. 4 (1893).

Pennington, Estill Curtis. *Look Away: Reality and Sentiment in Southern Art*. Atlanta, 1989.

Reeves, James F. *Gilbert Gaul*. Nashville, Tennessee, 1975.

Virginia Museum. *Painting in the South: 1564-1980*. Richmond, 1983.

**ARCHIVAL SOURCES**
Smithsonian Institution Fine Art Library, artist's vertical files.

**EXHIBITION HISTORY**
"Art and Artists of the South: The Robert Powell Coggins Collection," 1984-86. (See note on the catalog organization for complete exhibition schedule.)

# The Black Presence
# in Southern Painting

Prior to the Civil War, depictions of blacks in Southern art were fairly rare and most often confined to genre works of slave sales or portrait conversation groups in which black servants appeared with white families. A notable exception to this tradition occurred in New Orleans where several portraits of free people of color were painted, and remain extant.

Immediately before the war, the South Carolina artist William Aiken Walker began to create his scenes of Charleston street vendors and field hands. For more than fifty years, Walker's work typified that type of Southern genre painting that seems to mix the agenda of Barbizon naturalism with a patronizing affection. These works continue to perplex the sensitive student of art in an age when the tides of politically correct thinking threaten to overwhelm objective understanding.

However, with the beginning of this century, the black subject emerges as the focus of a strong counterculture movement in the South. Artists like Wayman Adams and John McCrady found genuine folkways in Southern black life that appealed to the modernist's longing for alternative solutions to an increasingly oppressive conformist society.

Undercurrents of racial tension will not vanish from American life overnight. Nor will the complex role of the black in Southern painting easily resolve itself in clear cultural dichotomies. It is a subject that demands continued study and reflection.

# THOMAS SATTERWHITE NOBLE

1835-1907

Born, Lexington, Kentucky; studied in Paris, France, with Thomas Couture, 1853; active in the Lexington/northern Kentucky area, 1855-1904; died, New York City.

## *The Price of Blood*

1868, signed and dated lower right
Oil on canvas, 39¼ x 49½ inches
1989.03.237

**PROVENANCE**
In the artist's possession until sold in 1875 to A.G. McDonald of Glasgow, Scotland; in passing; to Grand Central Galleries, New York; to Robert M. Hicklin, Jr., Inc., Spartanburg, South Carolina; by purchase to Southeastern Newspapers Corporation; by gift to Morris Museum of Art.

**LITERATURE**
Birchfield, James D., Albert Boime, and William J. Hennessey. *Thomas Satterwhite Noble 1835-1907.* Lexington, Kentucky, 1988. (This exhibition catalog contains Birchfield's essay, "The Artistic Career of Thomas Satterwhite Noble," which appeared in slightly different form in the *Kentucky Review* 6 (Winter and Summer 1986), and Boime's essay "Burgoo and Bourgeois: Thomas Noble's Images of Black People." Birchfield's notes contain critical bibliographic information on the full range of biographical and cultural context materials on Noble and his art.)

Boime, Albert. "Thomas Satterwhite Noble Casts Couture's Spell in America," in *Thomas Couture and the Eclectic Vision.* New Haven, Connecticut, 1980.

Garretson, Mary Noble Welleck. "Thomas S. Noble and his Paintings." *New York Historical Society Quarterly Bulletin* 24 (October 1940).

McElroy, Guy C. *Facing History: The Black Image in American Art 1710-1940.* Washington, D.C., 1988.

Pennington, Estill Curtis. *Look Away: Reality and Sentiment in Southern Art.* Atlanta, 1989.

**ARCHIVAL SOURCES**
Cincinnati Art Academy Archives.

Cincinnati Art Museum Library, artist's files, for unpublished biographical essay on Thomas S. Noble by Grace Noble Anderson.

**EXHIBITION HISTORY**
National Academy of Design, New York, 1868; Williams and Everett Gallery, Boston, October 1869; Pennsylvania Academy of Fine Arts, Philadelphia, 1869; First Cincinnati Industrial Exposition, August/September, 1870; Wiswell's Gallery, Cincinnati, April 1871; Third Cincinnati Industrial Exposition, 1872; James McClure and Sons, Glasgow, Scotland, 1875; "Look Away, Reality and Sentiment in Southern Art," Phillips Gallery, New York City, August 5-27, 1987; "Visions of America 1787-1987," ACA Gallery, New York City, September 30-October 24,

1987; "Thomas Satterwhite Noble 1835-1907," University of Kentucky Art Museum, April 10-May 29, 1988, Greenville County Museum of Art, Greenville, South Carolina, July 19-September 4, 1988, Art Academy of Cincinnati, September 18-November 6, 1988; "Facing History: The Black Image in American Art, 1710-1940," Corcoran Gallery of Art, Washington, D.C., and January 13-March 25, 1990, The Brooklyn Museum.

Much of the biographical literature attending Noble's life and training focuses upon his period of study with the French painter Thomas Couture. A superb technician, Couture was also a didactic history painter with a penchant for obscure allegorical symbolism. Learning from the master, Noble created several works where the obvious message is enhanced by the incorporation of mysterious semiotic notes into background, and, indeed, foreground, details.

Boime points out that the pile of money on the table is an extended metaphor based on the title. It is taken from Harriet Beecher Stowe's character Cassy, in *Uncle Tom's Cabin*, who, when shown the money obtained from the sale of her children by their cruel master, calls it "the price of their blood." On the rear wall, a print of the sacrifice of Isaac is another note of irony; seemingly no angel will stay this father's hand.

A precise triangularization isolates each of the individuals into non-interactive poses, at once the most obvious and most disturbing visual feature of the painting. The placid gentility of the mulatto son being sold into slavery contrasts with the callous slave trader and the eerie, arrogant stare of the master/father. Extended consideration of the image, in accord with nineteenth-century principles of "reading" a painting, establishes a fascinating purpose for each pose.

The slave trader represents the dispassionate capitalist, intent upon his job, impervious to moral judgment, indeed, even to the audience's gaze. He studies a new contract even as the torn fragments of another document lie mysteriously at the feet of the master, almost certainly symbolizing a failed promise of freedom. The cavalier pose of the mulatto son is the most seductive visual element in the painting: appealingly heroic, yet neither complaisant nor defiant.

# WILLIAM AIKEN WALKER

1838-1921

Born, Charleston, South Carolina; studied in Baltimore at the Maryland Institute, c. 1845-50; active in Charleston, South Carolina, Augusta, Georgia, New Orleans, and in various Southern resorts, including Arden, North Carolina, the Blue Ridge Mountains of Virginia, and Ponce Park, Florida, 1860-1919; died, Charleston.

## *Plantation Portrait*

1885, signed and dated lower left
Oil on canvas, 14 x 24 inches
1989.03.247

### PROVENANCE
From Marshall Hennis, Long Island, New York, to Robert M. Hicklin, Jr., Inc., Spartanburg, South Carolina; by purchase to Southeastern Newspapers Corporation; by gift to Morris Museum of Art.

### LITERATURE
Chambers, Bruce. *Art and Artists of the South.* Columbia, South Carolina, 1984.

Kelly, James C. *The South on Paper.* Spartanburg, South Carolina, 1985.

Mahe, John A.,II and Rosanne McCaffrey. *Encyclopedia of New Orleans Artists 1718-1918.* Historic New Orleans Collection, New Orleans, 1987.

McElroy, Guy C. *Facing History: The Black Image in American Art 1710-1940.* Washington, D.C., 1990.

Pennington, Estill Curtis. *Look Away: Reality and Sentiment in Southern Art.* Atlanta, 1989.

R.W. Norton Gallery of Art. *Louisiana Landscape and Genre Paintings of the 19th Century.* Shreveport, Louisiana, 1981.

Siebels, Cynthia. *The Sunny South: The Art of William Aiken Walker.* Unpublished manuscript in production with Saraland Press, Spartanburg, South Carolina.

Trovaioli, August P. and Roulhac B. Toledano. *William Aiken Walker, Southern Genre Painter.* Baton Rouge, Louisiana, 1972.

Virginia Museum. *Painting in The South: 1564-1980.* Richmond, 1983.

### ARCHIVAL SOURCES
Historic New Orleans Collection, artist's vertical files.

Howard-Tilton Memorial Library, Louisiana Collection, Tulane University, New Orleans.

During the late 1870s and early 1880s, Walker began to develop two formulaic approaches to painting for the trade, approaches that varied considerably in style and detail. Small (6-inch x 12-inch) paintings of cabin scenes were rendered for the resort trade and for New Orleans tourists. Larger works of the type seen here were more expensive and intended to appeal to a more sophisticated, wealthy clientele. Stylistic developments in these larger works culminated in the works issued as prints by the Currier & Ives firm between 1883 and 1885.

In most of these paintings, Walker divides the picture plane into three parallel settings. Behind a strongly defined foreground, often inhabited by workmen and overseers, one looks into a field of cotton with additional workers. At the rear of the picture plane, there are often minute outbuildings and the occasional steamboat, a highly desirable element.

Formalist analysis aside, the art of Walker continues to present problems for the social and cultural historian. Some, including Toledano and Trovaioli, see Walker as an American Barbizon painter, responding to black field hands in much the same way Millet responded to the gleaners of French wheat fields. Arguably, Walker is an accurate reporter of the existence of the black workers, creating realistic images of their lamentable plight. While some of his works, including this one, do, indeed, seem to be imbued with a familiar, benign paternalism, there are far too many others that employ caricature, making it difficult to completely trust or support his intent.

Still, ongoing public interest in his work and ambiguous levels of presentation ensure his place as one of the most important indigenous Southern painters of the nineteenth century.

## WAYMAN ADAMS

1883-1959

Born, Muncie, Indiana; studied at the John Herron Art Institute in Indianapolis, Indiana, 1900-1904; with William Merritt Chase in Florence in 1910, and with Robert Henri in Spain in 1912; active in New Orleans, 1916-1924 and during the 1930s; died, New York City.

### New Orleans Mammy

c. 1920, signed middle left

Oil on canvas, 50 x 40 inches

1989.01.001

**PROVENANCE**

Estate of the artist; to Berry-Hill Galleries, Inc., New York; by purchase to Robert Powell Coggins Collection; by purchase to Southeastern Newspapers Corporation; by gift to Morris Museum of Art.

**LITERATURE**

Chambers, Bruce. *Art and Artists of the South.* Columbia, South Carolina, 1984.

Earle, Helen L. *Biographical Sketches of American Artists.* Michigan State Library, 1924, reprinted, Charleston, South Carolina, 1972.

McElroy, Guy. *Facing History: The Black Image in American Art 1710-1940.* Washington, D.C., 1990.

Watson, E.W. "Wayman Adams Paints a Portrait." *Art Instruction* 3, no. 6 (June 1939).

**ARCHIVAL SOURCES**

Archives of American Art, Smithsonian Institution.

Historic New Orleans Collection, artist's vertical files.

New York Public Library, artist's vertical files.

Smithsonian Institution Fine Arts Library, artist's vertical files.

**EXHIBITION HISTORY**

"Art and Artists of the South: The Robert Powell Coggins Collection," 1984-1986. (See note on catalog organization for complete exhibition schedule.) "Facing History: The Black Image in American Art 1710-1940," Corcoran Gallery of Art, Washington, D.C., January 13-March 25, 1990, The Brooklyn Museum, April 20-June 25, 1990.

In an interview with the art historian DeWitt Clinton McClellan held July 1, 1926, in his studio in New York and now recorded in the Archives of American Art, Adams make a passing reference to having made his first trip to New Orleans in 1916. Thereafter, he "went there every year" for sketching and painting, either on his way to California, where he wintered during the years after the First World War, or to Mexico, where he often wintered in the decade of the 1930s at the artists' colony in San Miguel Allende.

Adams' brief mention of New Orleans is both tantalizing and frustratingly bare of articulated response to the steamy recherche´ environment of the Vieux Carre´. He was there, after all, during the same time that William Faulkner and Sherwood Anderson were writing near Jackson Square, and when artists in the local Arts and Crafts Club were nurturing indigenous Louisiana modernism.

However, if one considers the tremendous impact that Henri's example had upon Adams, *New Orleans Mammy* can be seen as a kind of atmospheric response to the possibilities of local color in the Crescent City. Adams balanced his lushly rendered "lighting portraits" of society types with painterly evocations of locals he encountered on his trips South and Southwest. These he kept for himself as a form of testament to higher ambition.

Claudia Vess' observation, in *Facing History,* that the portrait creates "a mood of pensive resignation" even as the artist creates a nostalgic link with "a role fulfilled by female plantation slaves," only partially captures elements of ambiguity in the artist's narrative intent. This is also a work in which the subject, regardless of color or social role, is presented with enormous dignity.

## ELEANORA GIBSON HOUSTON

1883-1942

Born, Richmond, Virginia; studied, Art Students League, with Kenneth Hayes Miller, 1905, and in Paris, France, 1907-09; active in Richmond throughout her life, especially with Adele Clark in the Academy of Sciences and Fine Arts and The Art Club; died, Richmond.

### *First Communion*

c. 1930
Oil on canvas, 28 x 34 inches
1989.01.081

Thomas Colt notes that Nora Houston was "a person of deep spiritual and social consciousness (who) worked fruitfully in the social field as well as in the field of art." The only surviving biographical materials, as well as the only list of her works, support that observation. She did, indeed, work to create art education programs in Richmond, and she often essayed individuals, black and white, in religious settings.

Consideration of *First Communion* does evoke the problematic issue of paternalistic white painters rendering black subject matter in fairly anonymous terms. Paternalism is not the most apparent visual intent in a work that captures the evanescent quality of white clad black children participating in an ancient rite of passage. Instead, it undoubtedly affirms the artist's belief in universal salvation. She was, writes Colt, one who "labored long and sympathetically for her fellowman in Virginia."

**PROVENANCE**
From the estate of the artist; to Gallery Mayo, Richmond, Virginia; to Robert M. Hicklin, Jr., Inc., Spartanburg, South Carolina; by purchase to the Robert Powell Coggins Collection; by purchase to Southeastern Newspapers Corporation; by gift to Morris Museum of Art.

**LITERATURE**
Colt, Thomas C., Jr. *Nora Houston. Virginia Artists Series,* no. 8. Virginia Museum, Richmond, 1940.

**ARCHIVAL SOURCES**
Center for the Study of Southern Painting, Morris Museum of Art.

Virginia Museum of Art, Fine Art Library, Richmond.

**EXHIBITION HISTORY**
"Women Artists from Richmond's Past," Gallery Mayo, Richmond, Virginia, March 23-May 5, 1984.

CARRIE STUBBS

Life circumstances unknown

*Charleston Bride*

1948, signed lower left
Oil on canvas, 36 x 25⅞ inches
1989.01.197

Inscribed, verso: "Charleston Bride 19-XII-48." The frustrating lack of information on this artist is further compounded by the excellent technical ability the work displays. Neither condescending nor patronizing, it is a work that represents certain lingering trends in larger American art that came of age during the Great Depression. At that time, the art of social concern and urban realism generated images of ordinary individuals going about their lives and work that transcended the narrative restrictions of traditional genre painting. This Charleston bride is not meant to be a player in some suggestive scene, merely an engrossing individual engaging the viewer with an honest and forthright gaze.

**PROVENANCE**
From Olaf Packer, New Jersey; to Robert M. Hicklin, Jr., Inc., Spartanburg, South Carolina; by purchase to Robert Powell Coggins Collection; by purchase to Southeastern Newspapers Corporation; by gift to Morris Museum of Art.

**LITERATURE**
Chambers, Bruce. *Art and Artists of the South.* Columbia, South Carolina, 1984.

**ARCHIVAL SOURCES**
Carolina Art Association, Gibbes Art Gallery, Charleston, South Carolina.

**EXHIBITION HISTORY**
"Art and Artists of the South": The Robert Powell Coggins Collection, 1984-1986. (See note on catalog organization for complete exhibition schedule.)

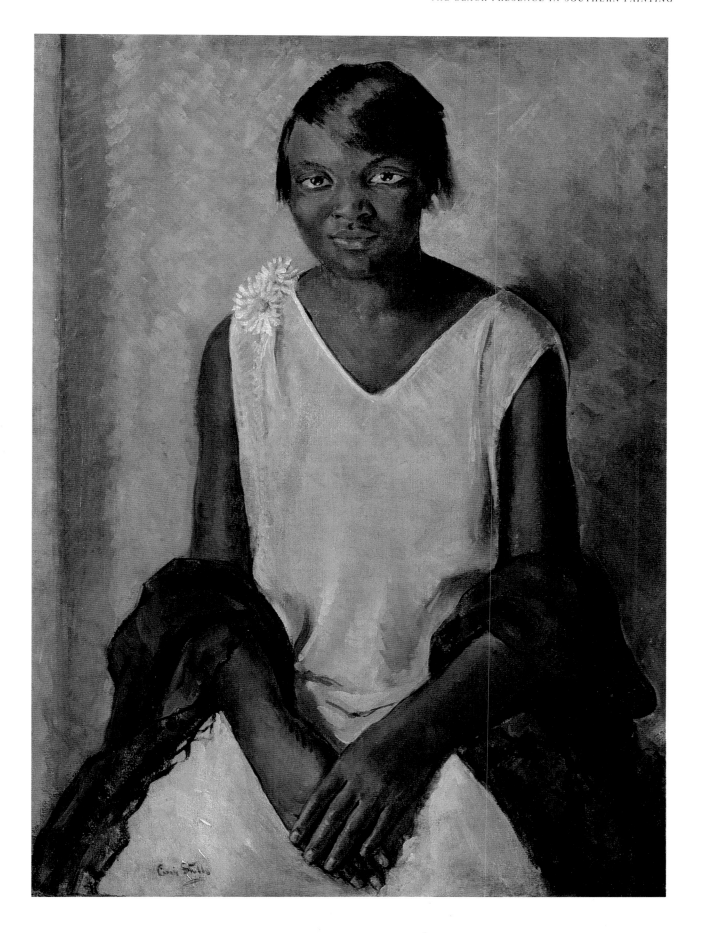

# Southern Still-Life Art

In the academic ordering of Western world art that arose in the eighteenth century, still-life painting placed last. The painting of exalted religious and historical subjects took precedence over the lowly, random, sometimes chaotic displays of fruits and flowers that intrigued the more defiant naturalists.

It is tempting to see the emergence of a genuinely accomplished and fully realized still-life tradition as a manifestation of certain protestant northern European ideologies. Mutability, the idea of change, is a metaphoric aspect of life well captured by the bounty of the earth. Flowers in full bloom, just about to drop their petals, and ripened fruit just on the verge of bruised decay, are "memento mori," fragrant reminders that all things must pass.

Just as the still-life tradition was slow to develop in the larger nation state, so it followed in the South. The great boom of still-life painting in America, in the heady days of antebellum prosperity, appropriated that theme of abundance that characterizes the natural prosperity of the subdued virgin wilderness.

In the South, that gracious plenty was quite lushly depicted by a wide range of artists. Some, like T. Addison Richards, brought a simple touch to the Georgia peach. Others, like Hal Morrison, found a fresh catch of fish and game the impetus to pleasing compositions.

# THOMAS ADDISON RICHARDS

1820-1900

Born, London, England; active in Penfield, Augusta, and Athens, Georgia, and in Charleston, South Carolina, 1838-1845; made frequent trips to the South collecting materials for travel writing and illustration, 1845-c. 1870; died, Annapolis, Maryland.

## Basket of Peaches

c. 1865, signed lower left
Oil on canvas, 14 x 12 inches
1989.01.160

The serenely composed restraint of Richards' basket of peaches represents a lingering affection for the American neo-classical approach to still-life art. Richards' contemporaries John Francis and Severin Rosen were creating larger, more lush works with those thematic suggestions of abundance and disorder that the mid-Victorians found so appealing. One would like to think these peaches were a visual tribute to Georgia, where Richards spent much of his youth and where he so often returned for inspiration in his writing and landscape art.

### PROVENANCE
From the artist's studio, after 1883; in passing; to Kennedy Gallery, New York; by sale to Bentley-Sellars Collection, Marietta, Georgia; by purchase to Robert Powell Coggins Collection; by purchase to Southeastern Newspapers Corporation; by gift to Morris Museum of Art.

### LITERATURE
Chambers, Bruce. *Art and Artists of the South.* Columbia, South Carolina, 1984.

. *Selections from the Robert P. Coggins Collection of American Painting.* Rochester, New York, 1976.

Gerdts, William H. and Russell Burke. *American Still-Life Painting.* New York City, 1971.

Griffith, Louis T. "T. Addison Richards: Georgia Scenes by a Nineteenth Century Artist and Tourist." *Georgia Museum of Art Bulletin* 1, no. 1 (1974).

Koch, Mary Levin. "The Romance of American Landscape: The Art of Thomas Addison Richards." *Georgia Museum of Art Bulletin* 8, no. 2 (1983).

Richards, Thomas Addison. *American Scenery.* New York City, 1854.

. *Appleton's Illustrated Handbook of American Travel.* New York City, 1857.

. "The Landscape of the South." *Harper's New Monthly* magazine 6 (May 1853).

. "The Rice Lands of the South." *Harper's New Monthly* magazine 17 (November 1859).

. *The Romance of the American Landscape.* New York City, 1855.

. *Summer Stories of the South.* New York City, 1853.

. *Tallulah and Jocasse.* New York City, 1852.

Richards, William Carey, and Thomas Addison Richards. *Georgia Illustrated.* Penfield, Georgia, 1842.

Rutledge, Anna Wells. "Artists in the Life of Charleston." *Transactions of the American Philosophical Society* 39, Philadelphia, (1950).

Virginia Museum. *Painting in the South: 1564-1980.* Richmond, 1983.

### ARCHIVAL SOURCES
National Academy of Design Library, New York City.

### EXHIBITION HISTORY
This work may be object shown by Richards at the National Academy of Design in 1865 and 1869, and at the Brooklyn Art Association, November 1883; "Selection from the Robert P. Coggins Collection of American Painting," The High Museum of Art, Atlanta, December 3, 1976-January 16, 1977, Memorial Art Gallery of the University of Rochester, Rochester, New York, February 25-April 10, 1977, Herbert F. Johnson Museum of Art, Cornell University, Ithaca, New York, May 4-June 12, 1977; "Art and Artists of the South: The Robert Powell Coggins Collection," 1984-1986. (See note on catalog organization for complete exhibition schedule.)

ANDREW JOHN HENRY WAY

1826-1888

*An Abundance of Fruit*

c. 1875, signed lower right
Oil on canvas, 22 x 30 inches
1989.08.288

Born in Washington, D.C.; studied with John P. Frankenstein in Cincinnati, and with Alfred Jacob Miller in Baltimore, before studying in France and Italy, 1850-1854; active in Baltimore throughout his career; died, Baltimore.

Way was the most prominent still-life artist working below the Mason-Dixon line in the years immediately before and after the Civil War. He was known primarily for his realistic renderings of varieties of grapes, which were often dramatically lit in glistening tones on a black background. This work departs from Way's antebellum approach to random still-life art in both composition and coloration. Way's earlier work is in the spirit of American abundant still-life art. Here we see a seemingly random group of fruits, flowers, and vegetables actually rather carefully composed. Note the collard leaf under the mid-ground, and the large Rockingham Majolica vase in the rear.

PROVENANCE
From a private collection in Baltimore to Colwill-McGehee Gallery, Baltimore; by purchase to Southeastern Newspapers Corporation; by gift to Morris Museum of Art.

LITERATURE
Blumenthal, Arthur R., ed. *350 Years of Art and Architecture in Maryland.* College Park, Maryland, 1984.

Gerdts, William H. and Russell Burke. *American Still-Life Painting.* New York City, 1971.

Gerdts, William H. *Painters of the Humble Truth: Masterpieces of American Still-Life 1801-1939.* Columbia, Missouri, 1981.

"Grapes from Mr. Walters' Greenhouse." *The Bulletin of the Walters Art Gallery* 3, no. 4 (January 1951).

Johnson, Sona K. *American Paintings 1750-1900, from the Collection of the Baltimore Museum of Art.* Baltimore, 1983.

Johnson, William R. "American Paintings in the Walters Art Gallery." *Antiques* 106 (November 1974).

King, Edward S. and Marvin C. Ross. *Catalog of the American Works of Art, The Walters Art Gallery.* Baltimore, 1956.

Pleasants, J. Hall. *250 Years of Painting in Maryland.* Baltimore, 1945.

Virginia Museum. *Painting in the South: 1564-1980.* Richmond, 1983.

Wiegand, Henry H. "The Charcoal Club of Baltimore." *Art and Archaeology* 19 (May-June 1925).

ARCHIVAL SOURCES
Maryland Historical Society Library, J. Hall Pleasants Collection, Annapolis.

Smithsonian Institution Fine Arts Library, artist's vertical files.

Walters Art Gallery Library, Baltimore.

## GEORGE COCHRAN LAMBDIN

### 1830-1878

Born, Pittsburgh; studied with his father, the artist James Reid Lambdin, and at the Pennsylvania Academy of Fine Arts; made frequent visits to Natchez, Mississippi; died, Germantown, Pennsylvania.

### *Roses*

c. 1880, Signed lower left
Oil on board, 22 x 14 inches
1992.025

### *Roses and Fuchsia*

c. 1880
Oil on board, 22 x 12 inches
1992.026

Though Lambdin never lived in the South, he had very strong ties to Natchez through his paternal uncle, Samuel Lambdin, a successful cotton planter. His father worked as an itinerant painter in the South and the family retained strong ties with their kinsman in Mississippi even after the great division of the war.

Gerdts and Burke have written that Lambdin was among the most important American still-life painters of his day. He developed a particular style, which, as we see here, featured brightly colored roses from his own garden displayed against a dark background, which set them off in a very effective manner. It was this quality that led Gerdts and Burke to declare that Lambdin "adds a new interest in light and in atmosphere to the still-life vocabulary, in line with luminist developments in American painting, and Impressionist, or proto-impressionist ones abroad. His flowers are beautifully drawn and painted, and they wave on long, graceful stems in a casual, sometimes crisscrossing arrangement. In keeping with this naturalness, there is no apparent formal ordering of the flowers, which range from buds to full blooms, though their placement and patterning are carefully chosen."

**PROVENANCE**
Christie's Auction No. 7414, Lot 41A, by purchase to Morris Museum of Art.

**LITERATURE**
Gerdts, William H. and Russell Burke. *American Still-Life Painting.* New York City, 1971.

Jelett, Edwin C. *Germantown Gardens and Gardeners.* Germantown, Pennsylvania, 1914.

Pennington, Estill Curtis. "The Kentucky-Mississippi Itinerancy," *The Southern Quarterly* (Fall 1986).

Weidner, Ruth Irwin. *George Cochran Lambdin 1830-1896.* Chadds Ford, Pennsylvania, 1986.

# HAL ALEXANDER COURTNEY MORRISON

1848 or 1852-1927

## *Trout*

c. 1910
Oil on canvas, 16 x 20 inches
On loan to the Morris Museum of Art
from the family of William S. Morris, III

Born, Prince Edward Island, Canada; active in Atlanta, Georgia, 1883-1918, in Auburndale, Florida, 1918-1926; died, Atlanta.

Most biographical accounts note that Morrison's favorite activities were painting and fishing, despite his having been trained at Harvard as a physician. It should come as no surprise, then, that Morrison was best known in Atlanta for his still-life works of fish and game. His frequent winter trips to Florida provided ample subject matter, and he sold large numbers of these paintings in the Atlanta area. The warm, rich coloration of this work has the look and feel of those late nineteenth-century chromolithographs that seem to have inspired Morrison's appeal to popular taste. Many of his Southern contemporaries in New Orleans, notably William Aiken Walker, George L. Viavant, Andres Molinary, Paul Poincy, and Achille Perelli, were sustained by the same market.

**PROVENANCE**
Discovered in Florida, acquired by the Robert Powell Coggins Collection; to Robert M. Hicklin, Jr., Inc., Spartanburg, South Carolina; by purchase to William S. Morris, III.

**LITERATURE**
Atlanta Historical Society. *Land of our Own: 250 Years of Landscape and Gardening Tradition in Georgia,* 1733-1983. Atlanta, 1983.

Chambers, Bruce. *Art and Artists of the South.* Columbia, South Carolina, 1984.

Crannell, Carlyn Gaye. *In Pursuit of Culture: A History of Art Activity in Atlanta, 1847-1926.* Unpublished Ph.D. dissertation, Emory University, Atlanta, 1981. (A copy may be found in the library of the Atlanta Historical Society.)

# ELLA SOPHONISBA HERGESHEIMER

1873-1943

## *Gladiolas in a Blue Vase*

c. 1930, signed lower left
Oil on canvas, 36 x 25 inches
1989.01.076

Born, Allentown, Pennsylvania; studied with William Merritt Chase and Cecilia Beaux at the Pennsylvania Academy of Fine Arts; active in Nashville, Tennessee, 1907-1943; died, Nashville.

Charles Wilson Peale's great-great-granddaughter seems to have inherited the Peale panache with a brush. Like her antecedents, Hergesheimer was an accomplished portraitist who could also create a tightly controlled still-life. The predominant aqua tonality of this work, combined with the large-scale, spare use of background detail and strong lighting, creates an art-deco effect in the precisionist mood.

**PROVENANCE**
Purchased in a Christie's East sale for the Robert Powell Coggins Collection; by purchase to Southeastern Newspapers Corporation; by gift to Morris Museum of Art.

**LITERATURE**
Burton, Vincent. "Some Portraits by Ella S. Hergesheimer." *International Studio* 37 (March 1909).

Kelly, James C. "Landscape and Genre Painting in Tennessee, 1810-1985." *Tennessee Historical Quarterly* 44, no. 2 (Summer 1985).

——. "Portrait Painting in Tennessee," *Tennessee Historical Quarterly* 46, no. 4 (Winter 1987).

Nashville Artist Guild Gallery. *Nashville Artists/Century II*. Nashville, Tennessee, 1980.

*Nashville Banner*. July 5, 1932, and February 21, 1938.

**EXHIBITION HISTORY**
"'Art and Artists of the South' and Recent Acquisitions," Georgia Museum of Art, University of Georgia, Athens, January 9-February 21, 1988.

# Landscape Painting in the South

Because the South has been predominantly an agrarian culture, one might expect a profoundly insightful landscape tradition to have emerged on the scene. But T. Addison Richards' lament in 1853 that "little has yet been said, either in picture or story, of the natural scenery of the South" is a telling commentary on the extent to which the artistic possibilities of that landscape were "known abroad or appreciated at home."

Curiously enough, it was a paymaster on a Union gunboat, Joseph Rusling Meeker, who first took up Richards' charge in the swamps and bayous of Louisiana. While on duty there, Meeker made extensive drawings of the scene, which he subsequently developed into a formulaic vocabulary of design. Many of Meeker's works achieve his self-expressed aim of an "area of repose" that leads the eye to a point of peace in an exotic setting.

Formulaic design does characterize much of Southern landscape art from the mid-nineteenth century until the Second World War. Artists like A.J. Drysdale in New Orleans and the Brenner family in Louisville, Kentucky, settled on interpretive modes for site-specific areas, which they perpetrated through a series of works. Many of these landscapes portend more than they portray, and leave the viewer gaping into a seductive setting just beyond reach.

# WILLIAM CHARLES ANTHONY FRERICHS

1829-1905

Born in Ghent; educated at the Royal Academy at The Hague, Netherlands; active in the area of Greensboro, North Carolina, 1855-1865; died, Tottenville, New Jersey.

## *Southern Mountain Landscape, North Carolina*

c. 1860, signed lower right
Oil on canvas, 32 x 47 inches
1989.01.059

Although this work has been exhibited as depicting a scene near Lake Toxaway, North Carolina, both the geological and historical circumstances surrounding that area make this site attribution unlikely. It also differs in style from the powerful slashing brush work in the Barbizon manner which Frerichs used to capture the energetic rush of the French Broad River. However, the painting is rendered in the spirit of international romanticism, expressing that profound regard for light in transition that, in American art studies, we have come to call luminism. This style was very prevalent during the antebellum period, and that fact, together with its discovery in a Southern locale, supports the idea that this work stems from Frerichs' Southern stay.

**PROVENANCE**

Discovered in a pawn shop near Columbia, South Carolina, by John George Walker; to Robert Powell Coggins Collection; by purchase to Southeastern Newspapers Corporation; by gift to Morris Museum of Art.

**LITERATURE**

Chambers, Bruce. *Art and Artists of the South.* Columbia, South Carolina, 1984.

Safford, Hildegarde J. and Benjamin F. Williams. W.C.A. Frerichs. Raleigh, North Carolina, 1974.

**EXHIBITION HISTORY**

"'Art and Artists of the South' and Recent Acquisitions," Georgia Museum of Art, University of Georgia, Athens, January 9-February 21, 1988; "Wishful Thinking: Victorian Themes in Southern Painting," Cheekwood, Nashville, Tennessee, December 7, 1991-February 2, 1992.

## LOUIS REMY MIGNOT

1831-1871

Born, Charleston, South Carolina; studied in the Netherlands, c. 1851; intermittent activity in South Carolina; died, Brighton, England.

### *Lowland Landscape with Deer*

c. 1860, signed lower left
Oil on canvas, 29 x 36 inches
Robert Powell Coggins Art Trust,
Morris Museum of Art COG-XX16

Alone of the artists under consideration in this section, Mignot achieved in his lifetime both renown and acceptance among the legendary Hudson River School of American landscape painters. Henry Tuckerman took special note of "the southern effects so remarkably rendered" by the artist, an ability which he attributes in part to his "nativity…." Katherine Manthorne has shown a particular sensitivity to Mignot's Southern origins as a source for his affinity with certain strains of international romanticism. "Mignot's South Carolina background contributed to that outlook," she asserts, for "he, in common with Southern writers and intellectuals of his day, looked to the English Romantics for models and inspiration."

**PROVENANCE**
From Kennedy Gallery, New York; to the Robert Powell Coggins Collection; to Robert Powell Coggins Art Trust, Morris Museum of Art.

**LITERATURE**
*Catalog of a Choice Collection of Paintings, and Studies from Nature, Painted by Louis R. Mignot.* New York City, 1862.

*Catalog of the Mignot Pictures with Sketch of the Artist's Life by Tom Taylor, Esq. and Opinions of the Press.* London and Brighton, England, 1876.

*Catalog Special Sale of Fine Oil Paintings Including the Collection of the Well-Known American Artist, Mr. L.R. Mignot, Now in London.* New York City, 1868.

Jentsch, Carol. "Louis Remy Mignot." *Florida Visionaries.* University Gallery, University of Florida, Gainesville, Florida, 1989.

Manthorne, Katherine. "Louis Remy Mignot." *American Paradise: The World of the Hudson River School.* Metropolitan Museum of Art, New York City, 1987.

. "Louis Remy Mignot's Sources of the Susquehanna." In Novak, Barbara and Annette Blaugrund, eds. *Next to Nature: Landscape Paintings from the National Academy of Design.* New York City, 1980.

Tuckerman, Henry T. *Book of the Artists: American Artist Life.* New York City, 1966, reprint of 1867 edition.

**ARCHIVAL SOURCES**
Smithsonian Institution Fine Arts Library, artist's files.

## MEYER STRAUS

1831-1905

*Bayou Teche*

c.1870, signed lower left
Oil on canvas, 30 x 60 inches
1989.03.239

Born, Germany; active in New Orleans, 1869-1872; died, San Francisco.

Between 1869 and 1872 Straus was "engaged by Messrs. Spalding and Bidwell as scenic artist for their great theatrical circuit ..." (New Orleans *Daily Picayune,* September 10, 1870) in which capacity he painted backdrops for major productions at the Academy of Music in New Orleans. One reviewer praises him for creating works "of an order of merit seldom presented" while noting it may not be generally known that Mr. Straus "is a landscape painter of decided genius" (*Daily Picayune,* April 7, 1872). That same ebullient notice mentions that Straus "has painted some Southern scenes" that "demonstrate one fact – that we need not go out of the Gulf States for that kind of sylvan beauty which ... is a perpetual source of pleasure to the eye." Be that as it may, Straus' reputation as a creator of "counterfeit presentment" implies that his vision of the swamp has far more in common with the footlights of theatrical settings than with an atmospheric response to a particular site. Even so, this is a most impressive work, whose resemblance to a backdrop is expanded by a strongly defined foreground and a distant, alluring background, overshadowed by monumental live oaks and hanging moss.

PROVENANCE
From the artist to the Hotel Del Monte, Monterey, California; by transfer to the Naval Post Graduate School, Hotel Del Monte, Monterey; by auction at Fort Ord, Monterey, to Charles Fisher, Monterey; by sale to Trotter Galleries, Pacific Grove, California; to Robert M. Hicklin, Jr., Inc., Spartanburg, South Carolina; by purchase to Southeastern Newspapers Corporation; by gift to Morris Museum of Art.

LITERATURE
Mahe, John A., II and Rosanne McCaffrey. *Encyclopedia of New Orleans Artists 1718-1918.* Historic New Orleans Collection, New Orleans, 1987.

Pennington, Estill Curtis. *Downriver: Currents of Style in Louisiana Painting 1800-1950.* Gretna, Louisiana, 1991.

Schwartz, Ellen. *San Francisco Art Exhibition Catalogs, A Descriptive Checklist and Index.* San Francisco, undated.

ARCHIVAL SOURCES
Historic New Orleans Collection, artist's files.

Works Progress Administration, New Orleans Artists Directory, New Orleans Museum of Art.

EXHIBITION HISTORY
San Francisco Art Association, March 1879; San Francisco Art Association, 1896; "Downriver: Currents of Style in Louisiana Painting, 1800-1950," New Orleans Museum of Art, November 10-December 30, 1990.

## GEORGE F. HIGGINS

Before 1859-after 1884

Place of birth unknown; active in Florida c. 1870-80; place of death unknown.

### *Palm Grove, Florida*

c. 1875
Oil on academy board, 13½ x 19½ inches
1990.118

Higgins' only paper trail consists of scant exhibition records in the Boston area from 1859-62 when he exhibited at the Athenaeum and again in 1873 and 1884 when he appears on general artist's census rolls. Works bearing his signature and depicting Florida subject matter continue to appear. He may not have been an active painter after 1884; as he does not appear among the Florida artists in the great boom period ushered in by the conjunction of Henry Morrison Flagler and Martin John Heade in 1883, so his works are seemingly among the earliest Florida landscape paintings. *Florida Cabin Scene,* previously in the Coggins Collection and illustrated in Chambers (p. 57), has a slightly rough, genre quality, considering the cabin and the rough composition of the shaggy setting. Both this work and a smaller one in the museum's collection display a masterful use of light in the luminist manner. Considering their scale, and the intense quality of light, they may have represented an effort on the artist's part to create a formula that could be marketed for tourists or a Northern Victorian audience intrigued by the tropics.

**PROVENANCE**
Robert Powell Coggins Collection; by purchase to Morris Museum of Art.

**LITERATURE**
Chambers, Bruce. *Art and Artists of the South.* Columbia, South Carolina, 1984.

## E.T.H. FOSTER

Life circumstances unknown

### *Evening on the French Broad*

1877, signed and dated lower right
Oil on canvas, 36½ x 54¾ inches
1989.03.235

The stretcher is inscribed, verso: "Evening on the French Broad, N.C." Apart from signing and dating this canvas, the artist has left no other information yet detected as to his, or her, identity. In both technique and site-specific observation, it is a work of considerable sophistication. Warmly colored, the painting displays an accurate use of vanishing perspective to suggest the depth of the French Broad, seen in contrast to the surrounding mountains. Considering the technical excellence of the work, the mysterious identity of the artist is all the more frustrating. While W.C.A. Frerichs made use of the French Broad in antebellum landscape works, painting activity in the area at the date of this work would have been much more unusual.

**PROVENANCE**
Discovered in Wisconsin by Joe Camardo of Milwaukee; to Robert M. Hicklin, Jr., Inc., Spartanburg, South Carolina; by purchase to Southeastern Newspapers Corporation; by gift to Morris Museum of Art.

**LITERATURE**
Pennington, Estill Curtis. *Look Away: Reality and Sentiment in Southern Art.* Atlanta, 1987.

**EXHIBITION HISTORY**
"Look Away," Phillips Gallery, New York, August 1987; Swan Coach House Gallery, Atlanta, January 1988; Madison-Morgan Cultural Center, Madison, Georgia, November 19, 1989-March 18, 1990.

## CARL CHRISTIAN BRENNER

1838-1888

### *Beech Trees*

c. 1880, signed lower left
Oil on canvas, 18 x 24¼ inches
1989.01.020

Born, Bavaria, Germany; studied in Germany with Philip Frolig; active in New Orleans, 1853, and in Louisville, Kentucky, 1853-1888; died, Louisville.

By his own account, (Louisville *Courier-Journal,* undated article, 1885, Filson Club Archives) once Brenner arrived in Louisville he began to paint the local beech trees with great enthusiasm. "I have passed and am passing my life in their study …," he informed the reporter. In so doing, Brenner joined the ranks of late nineteenth-century American tonalists, artists who created signature formulaic approaches to particular aspects of their local terrain. Most often these works were restricted to a limited palette, depending upon a tonal variation in color harmonics rather than an expansive palette in the earlier, romantic mode.

Brenner's work, like that of his Southern contemporaries Meeker, Drysdale, and Joiner, was offered to the public as a consistent form of landscape art, a consistency that critics, in his time and subsequently, found repetitious. Brenner responded to such charges quite frankly: "Art is long. Nature full of changes, and my theme, while it remains much the same, differs in details always" (Louisville *Courier-Journal,* December 17, 1878).

**PROVENANCE**
Discovered by Dave Knoke, Atlanta; to Robert Powell Coggins Collection; by purchase to Southeastern Newspapers Corporation; by gift to Morris Museum of Art.

**LITERATURE**
Bier, Justus. "Carl C. Brenner: A German-American Landscapist." *The German-American Review* (April 1951).

. "Brenner: Kentucky's Old Master." *Courier-Journal* magazine. January 12, 1947.

Henry, Betty M. *Biographical Extracts Relating to Prominent Artists of Louisville and Kentucky.* Louisville, Kentucky, 1939.

J.B. Speed Museum. *An Exhibition of Kentucky Paintings by Carl Christian Brenner.* Louisville, Kentucky, 1947.

Owensboro Museum of Fine Art. *The Kentucky Tradition in American Landscape Painting.* Owensboro, Kentucky, 1983.

Weber, Bruce and Arthur F. Jones. *The Kentucky Painter from the Frontier Era to the Great War.* University of Kentucky Art Museum, Lexington, 1981.

**ARCHIVAL SOURCES**
The Filson Club, artist's files, Louisville, Kentucky. (See also photo collections for copies of Kate Matthews' photographs of Brenner landscape painting sites.)

Louisville Free Public Library, artist's files. (See also Works Progress Administration, Louisville Library Collections Biography series.)

**EXHIBITION HISTORY**
"'Art and Artists of the South' and Recent Acquisitions," Georgia Museum of Art, University of Georgia, Athens, January 9-February 21, 1988.

# JOHN MARTIN TRACY

1843-1893

Born, Rochester, Ohio; studied at the Ecole des Beaux Arts in Paris, France, 1870; active in Ocean Springs, Mississippi, 1889-1893; died, Ocean Springs.

## A Field Trial – A Shot

c. 1885, signed lower right
Oil on canvas, 30 x 50 inches
1989.03.241

This work may have been among that group of paintings drawn together for "J.M. Tracy" at the Ehrich-Newhouse Galleries, Inc., New York City, April 7 - May 2, 1936. The catalog of that exhibition notes that "every important Tracy painting is a monument to a great dog or horse ..." and that "they remain household treasures of the foremost shooting families of America. ..." One of the works illustrated in the small catalog, *Quail Shooting on the St. James River, Va.* bears a great resemblance to this painting in compositional detail. In both works, black men wait patiently in the background while members of the so-called "foremost shooting families" pursue their sport. The black presence is a jarring punctuation of the composition, a reminder of social function and social role during the heyday of Robber Baron English affectation. From a formalist standpoint, the work itself is at once very painterly and redolent of the warm color harmonics of early fall.

**PROVENANCE**

From Knoedler Gallery, New York; to Mrs. Dorothy Thorne, Long Island, New York; to Gerald Wunderlich Gallery, New York; to Robert M. Hicklin, Jr., Inc., Spartanburg, South Carolina; by purchase to Southeastern Newspapers Corporation; by gift to Morris Museum of Art.

**LITERATURE**

Ehrich-Newhouse Galleries, Inc. *J. M. Tracy.* New York, 1936.

Lloyd, Freeman. "The Dog Pictures of Tracy: Great American Artist Stopped Doing Battle Scenes to Place Animals on Canvas." *The American Kennel Gazette* 53, no. 5 (May 1936).

**ARCHIVAL SOURCES**

Robert M. Hicklin, Jr., Inc., gallery archives, Spartanburg, South Carolina. (Original research by Cynthia Seibels.)

Smithsonian Institution Fine Arts Library, artist's files.

**EXHIBITION HISTORY**

"Look Away," Phillips Gallery, New York, August 1987, Swan Coach House Gallery, Atlanta, January 1988.

## JOSEPH RUSLING MEEKER

1827-1889

Born, Newark, New Jersey; studied at the National Academy of Design, 1845; active in Louisville, Kentucky, 1852-1859, active in Louisiana, 1861-1865; thought to have made intermittent sketching expeditions to the Mississippi Delta area, 1865-1875; died, St. Louis.

### *Bayou Landscape*

1886, signed and dated lower right
Oil on canvas, 18 x 27 inches
1990.125

This very late work by Meeker demonstrates the extent to which his mature works, in a more somber, tonalist mood, differed from his earlier, almost mystical evocations of the swamps and bayous of the lower Mississippi. Conventions from his entire body of work persist: the standing heron, the tonal contrasts between the trees in the background arranged to create what Meeker called "major and minor lights," and the swamp lilies dotted across the foreground.

**PROVENANCE**
From the artist to the O'Neil family of New York, and then by descent; to Babcock Galleries, New York City; by purchase to Southeastern Newspapers Corporation; by gift to Morris Museum of Art.

**LITERATURE**
Barter, Judith A. and Lynn E. Springer. *Currents of Expansion: Paintings in the Midwest, 1820-1940.* St. Louis Art Museum, 1977.

Brown, C. Reynolds. *Joseph Rusling Meeker: Images of the Mississippi Delta.* Montgomery Museum of Fine Arts, Montgomery, Alabama, 1981.

*Catalog of the St. Louis Mercantile Library Exhibition of Paintings.* St. Louis, 1871.

Chambers, Bruce. *Art and Artists of the South.* Columbia, South Carolina, 1984.

Mahe, John A., II and Rosanne McCaffrey. *Encyclopedia of New Orleans Artists 1718-1918.* New Orleans, 1987.

Meeker, Joseph Rusling. Opening Address at the St. Louis Art Society Annual Meeting. *The Western* (December 1878).

. "Some Accounts of the Old and New Masters." *The Western* (1878).

. "Turner." *The Western* (December 1877).

Pennington, Estill Curtis. *Downriver: Currents of Style in Louisiana Painting 1800-1920.* Gretna, Louisiana, 1991.

. *Look Away: Reality and Sentiment in Southern Art.* Atlanta, 1989.

Rathbone, Perry. *Mississippi Panorama.* St. Louis, 1950.

R.W. Norton Art Gallery. *Louisiana Landscape and Genre Paintings of the Nineteenth Century.* Shreveport, Louisiana, 1981.

. *Westward the Way.* St. Louis, Missouri, 1954.

Virginia Museum. *Painting in the South: 1564-1980.* Richmond, 1983.

Weber, Bruce and Arthur F. Jones. *The Kentucky Painter from the Frontier Era to the Great War.* University of Kentucky Art Museum, Lexington, 1981.

**ARCHIVAL SOURCES**
Missouri Historical Society, St. Louis.

# HENRY OSSAWA TANNER

1859-1937

Born, Pittsburgh; studied at the Pennsylvania Academy of Fine Arts with Thomas Eakins, 1880-1882; active in Georgia and North Carolina, 1887-1891; died, Trepied, France.

## *Georgia Landscape*

1889-1890, signed lower left
Oil on canvas, 17¾ x 32¼ inches
1989.01.201

From January 1889 to January 1891 Tanner lived in Atlanta, where he tried unsuccessfully to operate a "photography gallery and art room," (Mosby, et. al., p.38). He spent the summer of 1889 in Highlands, North Carolina, for his health, making photographs and sketching. Chambers posits (p.76) that this work "was probably painted in the Fall of 1889 after Tanner's return from Highlands." Sewell takes issues with this attribution, stating, "the painting now called *Georgia Landscape* might be a work entitled *Early November*, which Tanner showed at the Pennsylvania Academy of Fine Arts in January, 1889" (Mosby, et. al. p.85). Sewell's belief that the work "combined Tonalism's subtle light and color effects with touches of bravura painting" (p.83) is well taken. Whether or not the work is indeed Georgian, it does provide a link to the artist's brief Southern sojourn.

### PROVENANCE

From the artist to Bishop and Mrs. Joseph C. Hartzell; into the possession of Sammy J. Hardeman, Atlanta; by purchase to Robert Powell Coggins Collection; by purchase to Southeastern Newspapers Corporation; by gift to Morris Museum of Art.

### LITERATURE

"An Afro-American Painter Who Has Become Famous in Paris." *Current Literature and Art*, no.45 (October 1908).

Chambers, Bruce. *Art and Artists of the South*. Columbia, South Carolina, 1984.

Cole, Helen. "Henry O. Tanner, Painter." *Brush and Pencil* 6, no. 3 (June 1900).

Crannell, Carlyn Gaye. "Henry O. Tanner: Atlanta Interlude." *The Atlanta Historical Society Journal* 27, no. 4 (Winter 1983-84).

____. *In Pursuit of Culture: A History of Art Activity in Atlanta, 1847-1926*. Unpublished Ph.D. dissertation, Emory University, Atlanta, 1981.

Fauset, Jessie. "Henry Ossawa Tanner." *The Crises* 27 (April 1924).

Frederich Douglass Institute. *The Art of Henry O. Tanner*. National Collection of Fine Arts, Washington, D.C., 1969.

Hartigan, Lynda. *Sharing Traditions: Five Black Artists in Nineteenth-Century America*. National Museum of American Art, Washington, D. C., 1985.

Lester, William R. "Henry O. Tanner, Exile for Art's Sake." *Alexander's Magazine*, no. 72 (December 15, 1908).

MacChesney, Clara T. "A Poet-Painter of Palestine." *International Studio* 50, no. 197 (July 1913).

Mathews, Marcia M. *Henry Ossawa Tanner, American Artist*. Chicago, 1969.

Mosby, Dewey F., Darrel Sewell, and Rae Alexander-Minter. *Henry Ossawa Tanner*. Philadelphia Museum of Art, Philadelphia, 1991.

Scarborough, W.S. "Henry Ossian (*sic*) Tanner." *Southern Workmen* 31, no. 12 (December 1902).

Simon, Walter. *Henry O. Tanner: A Study of the Development of An American Negro Artist*. Unpublished Ph.D. dissertation, New York University, 1961.

Tanner, Henry Ossawa. "Effort." *Exhibition of Religious Paintings by H.O. Tanner*. Grand Central Art Galleries, New York, 1924.

____. "The Story of An Artist's Life, Parts I and II." *The World's Work* 18, nos. 2 and 3 (June and July 1909).

Woodruff, Hale. "My Meeting with Henry O. Tanner." *The Crises* 77 (January 1970).

Woods, Naurice Frank, Jr. *The Life and Work of Henry O. Tanner*. Unpublished Ph.D. dissertation, Columbia Pacific University, 1987.

### EXHIBITION HISTORY

"Atlanta Collects," Trosby Auction Galleries, Atlanta, April 27-May 1, 1980. "Art and Artists of the South: the Robert Powell Coggins Collection" 1984-1986. (See note on catalog organization for complete exhibition schedule.) "Regional American Art," Greenville County Museum of Art, Greenville, South Carolina, November 1-December 31, 1990; "Henry Ossawa Tanner," Philadelphia Museum of Art, January 20-April 14, 1991, Detroit Institute of Arts, May 12-August 4, 1991, High Museum of Art, Atlanta, September 17-November 12, 1991, The Fine Arts Museums of San Francisco, M.H. de Young Memorial Museum, December 14, 1991-March 1, 1992.

# GEORGE DAVID COULON

1822-1904

Born, Seloncourt, France; arrived in New Orleans, 1833; studied with
Toussaint Bigot and Francoise Fleishbien, 1836; active in New Orleans
throughout his career; died, New Orleans.

## *Italian Caprice*

1895
Oil on canvas, 34 x 61 inches
1990.113

Coulon delighted in painting imaginary scenes that had absolutely
nothing to do with any landscape he had ever seen. Oblivious to
more earnest nineteenth-century concerns about "truth in art,"
Coulon happily copied prints of old masters and sites he had
never seen … such as George Washington's grave. Only in the
aftermath of his son's long journey through the swamps and
bayous did he attempt a realistic scene, of Bayou Beauregard, and
this was a great success, which regrettably, he did not repeat. In
this very late work, Coulon demonstrates his great technical
ability to absorb the visual aesthetics of the past with great
flourish. *Italian Caprice* recalls the campagna painting tradition
and the panoramic vistas of Claude Lorraine.

PROVENANCE
Dave Knoke, Atlanta; to Robert Powell Coggins Collection; to Robert Powell Coggins
Art Trust; by purchase to Morris Museum of Art.

LITERATURE
Bonner, Judith Hopkins. "George David Coulon: Painter." *In Old New Orleans*. Jackson,
Mississippi, 1983.

. "Artists' Associations in Nineteenth Century New Orleans: 1842-1860."
*The Southern Quarterly* 24, nos. 1 and 2 (Fall-Winter 1985).

. "Arts and Letters: An Illustrated Periodical of Nineteenth Century New Orleans."
*The Southern Quarterly* 27, no. 2 (Winter 1989).

Fulton, Joseph W. and Roulhac B. Toledano. "New Orleans Landscape Painting of the
Nineteenth Century." *Antiques* 93 (April 1968).

Mahe, John A., II and Rosanne McCaffrey. *Encyclopedia of New Orleans Artists
1718-1918.* Historic New Orleans Collection, New Orleans, 1987.

Pennington, Estill Curtis. *Downriver: Currents of Style in Louisiana Painting
1800-1950.* Gretna, Louisiana, 1991.

. *Look Away: Reality and Sentiment in Southern Art.* Atlanta, 1989.

## ARCHIVAL SOURCES

Historic New Orleans Collection, artist's files.

Louisiana State Museum Library. (Scrapbook 100 contains the manuscripts, in
Coulon's hand, of a brief autobiography and "Old Painters in New Orleans," both
composed at the request of New Orleans artist Bror Wikstrom.)

## EXHIBITION HISTORY

"Wishful Thinking: Victorian Themes in Southern Painting," Cheekwood, Nashville,
Tennessee, December 7, 1991-February 2, 1992.

# HARVEY JOINER

1852-1932

Born, Charlestown, Indiana; studied in St. Louis, 1874 with David (?) Hoffman; active in Louisville, Kentucky, 1880-1932; died, Louisville.

## *Wooded Landscape*

c. 1900, signed lower right
Oil on canvas, 28 x 40 inches
1989.08.287

Joiner was part of that large group of late nineteenth-century Louisville, Kentucky, artists, including the Brenner family, John Botto, and Clarence Boyd, who specialized in formula landscapes of the local setting. Joiner's most familiar work represents a winding road through local Cherokee Park, over which trees, with bright chartreuse leaves brushed in a thin staccato manner, loom. This work is thought to be the largest, most detailed, and certainly most accomplished painting from the artist's brush. Perhaps taking a cue from Carl Brenner, Joiner has created a fully realized scene of a wooded stream, with a well-handled sense of depth and perspective and tightly controlled green color harmonics.

**PROVENANCE**
Discovered in an auction at Butterfield's, San Francisco, 1989; by purchase to Steven Harvey; to Clifton Anderson, Lexington, Kentucky; by purchase to Southeastern Newspapers Corporation; by gift to Morris Museum of Art.

**LITERATURE**
Owensboro Museum of Fine Art. *The Kentucky Tradition in American Landscape Painting*. Owensboro, Kentucky, 1983.

Weber, Bruce and Arthur F. Jones. *The Kentucky Painter from the Frontier Era to the Great War*. University of Kentucky Art Museum, Lexington, 1981.

**ARCHIVAL SOURCES**
The Filson Club, Louisville, Kentucky, artist's files.

Louisville Free Public Library, artist's files. (See also Works Progress Administration, Louisville Library Collections Biography series.)

**EXHIBITION HISTORY**
"Wishful Thinking: Victorian Themes in Southern Painting," Cheekwood, Nashville, Tennessee, December 7, 1991-February 2, 1992.

## ELLIOTT DAINGERFIELD

1859-1932

Born, Harper's Ferry, Virginia; studied in New York with Walter Satterlee and at the Art Students League, 1880-1884; active in Fayetteville, North Carolina, before 1880, and in Blowing Rock, North Carolina, 1885-1932; died, New York.

### *Sunset Glory*

c.1915
Oil on canvas, 27½ x 33¾ inches
1990.014

Daingerfield was a very thoughtful artist who wrote and curated exhibitions even as he worked quite hard as a painter. His appreciation for Inness and Blakelock was highly unusual, considering the great success of the first and the sad personal failure of the second. *Sunset Glory* marks a departure from Daingerfield's more typical approach to landscape art. As a painter, he reflected "the essential Tonalist aesthetic of poetic conception based on memory, intimate personal style, and enriched colors, which represent a mood rather than a specific locale," to quote Diana Sweet. Yet in this work, we see not only a personal response to the Blowing Rock, North Carolina, mountains but also a full-blown luminist concern with light expressly brushed in a heavily impastoed, then flattened, style.

**PROVENANCE**

Richard York Gallery, New York; by purchase to Southeastern Newspapers Corporation; by gift to Morris Museum of Art.

**LITERATURE**

Berry-Hill Galleries, Inc. *Elliott Daingerfield: American Mystic (1859-1932).* New York City, 1983.

Chambers, Bruce. *Art and Artists of the South.* Columbia, South Carolina, 1984.

Corn, Wanda. *The Color of Mood: American Tonalism, 1880-1910.* San Francisco, de Young Museum, 1972.

Daingerfield, Elliott. *Catalog of a Loan Exhibition of Important Works by George Inness, Ralph Blakelock and Alexander Wyant.* Chicago, 1913.

    . *Fifty Paintings by George Inness.* New York, 1913.

    . *George Inness: The Man and His Art.* New York City, 1911.

    . "Henry Ward Ranger, Painter." *Century* magazine 97 (November 1918).

    . "Nature vs. Art." *Scribner's* magazine 49 (February 1911).

    . *Ralph Albert Blakelock.* New York, 1914.

    . "Ralph Albert Blakelock." *Art in America* 2 (December 1914).

Gerdts, William H., Diana Dimodica Sweet, and Robert R. Preato. *Tonalism, An American Experience.* New York City, 1982. (Contains excellent bibliography on tonalism.)

Hobbs, Robert. *Elliott Daingerfield Retrospective Exhibition.* Mint Museum, Charlotte, North Carolina, 1971.

Virginia Museum. *Painting in the South: 1564-1980.* Richmond, 1983.

**ARCHIVAL SOURCES**

Archives of American Art, Smithsonian Institution.

Center for the Study of Southern Painting, Morris Museum of Art. (Photographs of the artist and his family, and materials relating to Daingerfield's mural work in New York City.)

Smithsonian Institution Fine Arts Library, artist's files.

# Southern Impressionism

European impressionism springs from two parallel searches extending through the world of nineteenth-century art: an ongoing search for technical innovation, evolving along somewhat predictable lines, and a far more revolutionary search for subject matter more exotic, and more real, than academic.

However, what was a genuine revolt in Europe, ripe with controversy flung in the face of an overbearing establishment, became far more tame in America. Here, impressionism was transformed into an expressionistic style filling a vacuum in an art world devoid of national standards. Southern impressionism is a genteel movement, employing a revolutionary technique to present proper people in fragile settings, gazing tentatively out of the picture plane, caught in the midst of quiet, tentative situations. Genteel impressionism is a conceptual style that matches the Southern self-image in the late-nineteenth and early-twentieth centuries.

It was the perfect mode to convey a misty world of moonlight and magnolias, the world being fabricated by the apologist writers of the New South. Thomas Nelson Page laments that Southern history has a future "veiled in mist." Southern impressionism, which lingered long in the canon of Southern art, captures a mist that both obscures and enhances a world passing from romantic past to an uncertain future.

## GEORGE WOLTZE

Active in New Orleans, 1889

### *The Sunny South*

c. 1889
Oil on canvas, 28 x 39 inches
1990.124

Relatively little is known about Woltze other than his activity in New Orleans in 1889, painting various genre scenes in watercolor in the French Quarter. Compositional format in those works led Dr. David Driscoll of the Babcock Galleries to attribute this work to Woltze. That attribution may be supported by internal architectural elements and the presentation of the genre subject matter. The setting recalls the interior courts and patios of New Orleans, while the black subject with musical instrument was a frequent type in Southern art. One might see the strong sunlight and flowering vegetation as evidence of a Southern climate.

Woltze has created an enchanting work, with a theatrical, frontal composition relieved by vivid color and a gently amusing air. The black subject is not treated as a harsh caricature but as an amiable characterization well integrated into the scene. Still, the perky, alert dog arrests the scene with its penetrating silent stare, a point of rapt attention in a tranquil setting.

**PROVENANCE**
Christie's sale; by purchase to Babcock Galleries, New York; by purchase to Southeastern Newspapers Corporation; by gift to Morris Museum of Art.

**LITERATURE**
Mahe, John A., II and Rosanne McCaffrey. *Encyclopedia of New Orleans Artists 1718-1918.* Historic New Orleans Collection, New Orleans, 1987.
*Old Print Shop Portfolio* (October 1946).

**ARCHIVAL SOURCES**
Historic New Orleans Collection.

## ELLSWORTH WOODWARD

1861-1939

Born, Seekonk, Massachusetts; studied Rhode Island School of Design, 1878-1880, and in Munich, Germany, 1884; active in New Orleans, 1885-1939; died, New Orleans.

### *Portrait of Tony*

c. 1888
Oil on linen, 18 x 15 inches
1989.05.269

While certain similarities exist in the sources and early works of the two Woodward brothers, Ellsworth and William, it is important to note that Ellsworth's ultimate training came from the Munich Academy. Unlike its French equivalents, the Munich style was darker, stressing the emergence of light from shadow, and the use of deep brushstroke and palette knife application. Woodward was primarily known as a watercolorist, at any rate, and oils by him are somewhat rare. This work is even rarer because there does exist a charcoal sketch for this painting, formerly in the Nelson Collection of Baton Rouge. In the Munich tradition, Woodward has created a work that is a penetrating essay in character rather than an exercise in form and color.

Woodward was also an educator and museum official with very advanced ideas about the role of art in the South. These were articulated in an unpublished lecture he gave at the then-Delgado Museum of Art in New Orleans during the late 1920s. "…if the observer keeps steadily in view the fact that art is not a commodity, but a vehicle of expression intended to convey what goes on in the mind of the artist reacting to life, he cannot fail to be impressed with recent Southern work. There is in this work a lessening volume of traditional, sentimental, and tritely objective painting, and a growing volume of adventurous struggle toward the expression of ideas and the interpretation of nature and life."

**PROVENANCE**
From the artist to Carl Woodward; to the Nelson Collection, Baton Rouge, Louisiana; to Downtown Gallery, New Orleans; by purchase to Southeastern Newspapers Corporation; by gift to Morris Museum of Art.

**LITERATURE**
Barkemeyer, Estelle. *Ellsworth Woodward: His Life and Work.* Unpublished master's thesis, Tulane University, New Orleans, 1942.

Cullison, William R., III. *Two Southern Impressionists: An Exhibition of the Work of the Woodward Brothers, William and Ellsworth.* Art Collection of Tulane University, New Orleans, 1984.

Keyes, Donald. *Impressionism and the South.* Greenville County Museum of Art, Greenville, South Carolina, 1988.

Louisiana State University Union Art Committee. *Louisiana Artists from the Collection of Dr. and Mrs. James W. Nelson.* Baton Rouge, 1968.

Mahe, John A., II and Rosanne McCaffrey. *Encyclopedia of New Orleans Artists 1718-1918.* Historic New Orleans Collection, New Orleans, 1987.

Ormond, Suzanne and Mary E. Irvine. *Louisiana's Art Nouveau: The Crafts of the Newcomb Style.* Gretna, Louisiana, 1976.

Pennington, Estill Curtis. *Downriver: Currents of Style in Louisiana Painting 1800-1950.* Gretna, Louisiana, 1991.

Poesch, Jessie. *Newcomb Pottery: An Enterprise for Southern Women, 1895-1940.* Exton, Pennsylvania, 1984.

Virginia Museum. *Painting in the South: 1564-1980.* Richmond, 1983.

Woodward, Ellsworth. "Advice to the South." *Art Digest* 10 (December 1935).

**ARCHIVAL SOURCES**
Historic New Orleans Collection, artist's files.

Howard-Tilton Memorial Library, Special Collections and Collections, Tulane University, New Orleans.

Works Progress Administration Papers, New Orleans Museum of Art. (Contains manuscript copies of major lectures on art and art education delivered by Woodward during the 1930s.)

## VIRGINIA RANDALL McLAWS

1872-1967

Born, Savannah, Georgia; studied, Charcoal Club, Baltimore, and Pennsylvania Academy of Fine Arts, 1899-1903; active, and taught, at Sweet Briar College, Virginia, 1908-1938; died, Savannah.

### *Self Portrait at Easel*

c. 1910
Oil on canvas, 16 x 20¼ inches
Robert Powell Coggins Art Trust,
Morris Museum of Art COG-0028

The art of Virginia Randall McLaws is a tribute to certain enduring ideas about art and education in the South during the late nineteenth century. As the daughter of a Confederate general, Lafayette McLaws, the artist was raised in a world where her only options were to marry, to teach, or to be a quiet dependent upon the kindness of relatives. She met this situation with considerable grace, teaching at Sweet Briar while painting a series of modestly charming works in the impressionist style.

Like Catherine Wiley and Helen Turner, she may be described as a "genteel impressionist" and an artist whose work looks back to the joyous color values of French Impressionism as a source, rather than a challenge. In this work, the gray and mauve shadows and the broad painterly brush strokes achieve a tidy, pleasant essay on one of her favorite scenes, the rural campus of Sweet Briar College, Virginia, where she was a much beloved figure. Sitting outdoors, painting en plein air, she does achieve a delightful depth of field, balancing the strong, direct sunlight, with the pale mauve-gray shadows beneath the trees.

**PROVENANCE**
From the artist by inheritance to her niece, Mrs. King, Savannah, Georgia; to Terry Lowenthal, Savannah; to Robert Powell Coggins Collection; to Robert Powell Coggins Art Trust, Morris Museum of Art.

**LITERATURE:**
Sweet Briar College. "Virginia Randall McLaws - Algernon Sydney Sullivan Award." *Alumnae News* (December 1938).
    . "Virginia Randall McLaws Honored." *Alumnae News* (June 1941).

**ARCHIVAL SOURCES**
Sweet Briar College Archives, Sweet Briar, Virginia.

## PAUL SAWYIER

1865-1917

Born, Madison County, Ohio; studied at the Cincinnati Art Academy with Thomas S. Noble, 1884, and at the Art Students League in New York City with William Merritt Chase, 1889-1890; active, Frankfort, Kentucky, 1890-1908, and in Nelson and Jessamine Counties, Kentucky, 1908-1913; died, Catskill, New York.

### *Kentucky River Valley*

c. 1910, signed lower right
Oil on academy board, 14 x 17 inches
1989.04.254

Though relatively unknown outside the Bluegrass state, Sawyier remains the most wildly popular indigenous artist in the history of Kentucky. His warmly colored watercolors and oils capture much of the glowing spirit of the charming Kentucky landscape, especially the central Kentucky region in the vicinity of Elkhorn Creek in Franklin County. As a student at the Art Students League, Sawyier was deeply influenced by William Merritt Chase. As with Childe Hassam, many of his works have a uniform light quality that tends to dissolve form into glowing color abstractions. While not an atmospheric impressionist in any sense, he does bring a considerable sensitivity of spirit, if not place, to his works.

Keyes' observation that Sawyier's "simple, easy-to-comprehend compositional spaces generally do not contain the ambiguities and complexities found in other impressionist paintings" (p. 37) may be applied to the painting at hand. Still, while this work may be an ingenuous effort in color harmonics in full sunlight, it is not to be undervalued. Art Jones has remarked that the intellectual climate in which Sawyier functioned "could suggest close ties between impressionist writers and painters in Kentucky…" (p. 87). How true, and how intriguing to think of Sawyier working in the same vein as John Fox, Jr. and James Lane Allen to capture the glorious beauty of old Kentucky.

#### PROVENANCE
William Barrow Floyd, Lexington, Kentucky; by purchase to Southeastern Newspapers Corporation; by gift to Morris Museum of Art.

#### LITERATURE
Hamel, Mary Michael. *A Kentucky Artist: Paul Sawyier (1865-1917)*. Fred P. Giles Gallery, Eastern Kentucky University, Richmond, 1975.

Jones, Arthur. *The Art of Paul Sawyier*. Lexington, Kentucky, 1976. (Although this volume has no bibliography, the notes provide excellent sources on primary and secondary Sawyier materials.)

———. *Regional Impressionism in Kentucky: The Art of Paul Sawyier*. Ph.D. dissertation, Case Western Reserve University, Cleveland, Ohio, 1974.

Jillson, Willard Rouse. "A Bibliography of Paul Sawyier, American Artist." *Register of the Kentucky State Historical Society* 37 (October 1939).

———. *A Chronology of Paul Sawyier*. Frankfort, Kentucky, 1966.

———. *Paul Sawyier: American Artist (1865-1917), A Brief Biographical Sketch*. Lexington, Kentucky, 1961.

———. *Paul Sawyier and His Paintings: Centennial Exhibition 1865-1965*. J.B. Speed Memorial Museum, Louisville, Kentucky, 1965.

Keyes, Donald. *Impressionism and the South*. Greenville County Museum of Art, Greenville, South Carolina, 1988.

Townsend, John Wilson. "Paul Sawyier, Kentucky Artist: Some Recollections of Him." *Filson Club Quarterly* 33 (1959).

Weber, Bruce and Arthur F. Jones. *The Kentucky Painter from the Frontier Era to the Great War*. University of Kentucky Art Museum, Lexington, 1981.

#### ARCHIVAL SOURCES
Filson Club, Louisville, Kentucky, artist's files.
Kentucky Historical Society, Frankfort. (Sawyier family scrapbook, begun June 23, 1896.)

University of Kentucky, Margaret I. King Library, Special Collections, Lexington. (Correspondence and a group of site photographs taken by Sawyier in 1886.)

University of Louisville, Kentucky, Bridwell Art Library, Hite Art Institute. (Willard R. Jillson's personal papers, including preparatory notes for his publications on Sawyier, and transcripts of various interviews with individuals who knew Sawyier, as well as the manuscript of Lillian Sawyier Hill's *My Memories*.)

HELEN TURNER

1858-1958

Born, Louisville, Kentucky; studied, Artists Association of New Orleans, with Bror Wikstrom and Andres Molinary, 1886-1893, and at the Art Students League with Kenyon Cox and William Merritt Chase, 1895-1899; active in New Orleans, 1880-1893, and 1926-1949; died, New Orleans.

*A Long Time Ago*

1918
Oil on canvas, 17¾ x 23¾ inches
1989.05.265

Turner was well taught and taught well. As a young woman she studied with Andres Molinary in the Artists Association of New Orleans. Later she painted with the great American impressionist masters in the Art Students League in New York, an experience that she refined in the stylistic development of her own palette knife technique. As a mature artist she, herself, taught art classes at the New York YWCA. While impressionist in feel, her works do not recall the strong colorations of the first generation impressionists, French or American. They more nearly resemble the low-keyed domestic interiors of Vuillard. Keyes' observation that "women seldom mix with men and never appear in a crowd" (p. 42) has a certain literal truth whose psychological significance should not be overstated. As in the work at hand, Turner is creating a visual essay of form and mood founded in subdued color, and a passive, indirect light. From a literary perspective, it is questionable whether her women are any more isolated than many of their peers in the hierarchic environment of the late nineteenth century. This was not an isolation that affected Turner, who like Mary Cassatt, had an active and highly successful career.

**PROVENANCE**
Purchased from the artist for the New Orleans Museum of Art by the Lacoste Fund; deaccessed and sold, 1965, to Dr. Robert Smythe, New Orleans; to Keith Marshall, Madewood Plantation, Louisiana; by purchase to Southeastern Newspapers Corporation; by gift to Morris Museum of Art.

**LITERATURE**
Keyes, Donald. *Impressionism in the South.* Greenville County Museum of Art, Greenville, South Carolina, 1988.

Mahe, John A., II and Rosanne McCaffrey. *Encyclopedia of New Orleans Artists 1718-1918.* Historic New Orleans Collection, New Orleans, 1987.

Mount, May W. *Some Notables of New Orleans: Biographical and Descriptive Sketches of the Artists of New Orleans, and their Work.* New Orleans, 1896.

Rabbage, L.H. *Helen M. Turner, N.A. (1858-1958).* Cragsmoor Free Library, Cragsmoor, New York, 1983.

**ARCHIVAL SOURCES**
Cragsmoor Free Library, artist's vertical files, Cragsmoor, New York.

Historic New Orleans Collection, artist's files.

# ELIOT CLARK

1883-1980

Born, New York City; studied with his father, the tonalist painter Walter Clark; active in Savannah, Georgia, 1922-24, and in Albemarle County, Virginia, 1934-1980; died, Charlottesville, Virginia.

## Savannah Harbor

c. 1924, signed lower left
Oil on canvas, 20¼ x 24¼ inches
1990.028

In the manuscript of a biography of Eliot Clark, now on file with the Archives of American Art, Margaret Fowler Clark, the artist's second wife, recounts the impact Savannah had upon his art. Clark spent two winters, 1922 and 1923, in Savannah, where he had been invited to teach at the Savannah Art Club. "The interlude was delightful. The picturesque city with its silvery southern light, its many gardens, and ancient live oaks hung with gray Moss, enchanted Eliot. During those Savannah winters he painted many of his finest works, the waterfront at twilight, old homes and landmarks, marvelous great trees, colorful warehouses in the half-light and so on."

Considering the influence Clark's father, the tonalist Walter Clark, had upon his art, it is not surprising that *Savannah Harbor* is a tonalist endeavor in shades of mauve and gray with strong overtones of J.A.M. Whistler. Like Whistler, Clark has focused upon the harmonic values of colors in close proximity, which enhances depth and perspective as seen from the strongly frontal viewpoint of the balcony. As with Whistler's Valparaiso Harbor series, painterly horizontal brushstrokes expand the sense of rippling line, acting as a shimmering foil for the "half-light" Mrs. Clark conjures up. When Clark's series of Savannah paintings was exhibited in that city in 1925, the local art critic, Jane Judge, writing for the *Savannah Morning News*, March 17, 1925, perceived the association with Whistlerian harmonics, speaking of his art as "rich in color and harmonious in form."

### PROVENANCE
Purchased at a Sotheby's Arcade sale in Summer 1989, by Robert M. Hicklin, Jr., Inc., Spartanburg, South Carolina; by purchase to Southeastern Newspapers Corporation; by gift to Morris Museum of Art.

### LITERATURE
Clark, Eliot. *History of the National Academy of Design, 1825-1953.* New York City, 1954.

Keyes, Donald. *Impressionism and the South.* Greenville County Museum of Art, Greenville, South Carolina, 1988.

Love, Richard H. *Walter Clark (1848-1917) and Eliot Clark (1883-1980): A Tradition in American Painting.* R.H. Love Galleries, Chicago, 1980.

Pisano, Ronald G. *Eliot Clark: American Impressionist 1883-1980.* Hammer Galleries, New York City, 1981.

University of Virginia Art Museum. *Eliot Clark, N.A. Retrospective Exhibition.* Charlottesville, Virginia, 1975.

### ARCHIVAL SOURCES
Archives of American Art, Smithsonian Institution. (Contains the complete bibliography and manuscripts of Clark's extensive articles on American and oriental art.)

National Academy of Design, New York City.

### EXHIBITION HISTORY
Possibly included with an exhibition of Clark's works held at the Telfair Academy of Arts and Sciences, Savannah, Georgia, March 16-April 6, 1925.

# CATHERINE WILEY

1879-1958

Born, Coal Creek, Tennessee; studied at the Art Students League 1903-1905 with Frank Vincent Dumond and Howard Pyle, and with Robert Reid, 1912; active in Knoxville 1905-1925, died, Philadelphia, Pennsylvania.

*Tennessee Landscape*

c. 1921
Oil on canvas, 18 x 12 inches
1990.068

Catherine Wiley struggled quite valiantly for more than twenty years to overcome her rural Southern background and break into the mainstream of American art circles. Despite winning several regional prizes, she was rejected by the National Academy of Design on several occasions between 1915 and 1925. Some in her family believed these rejections led to her ultimate mental collapse.

Her works have the same accomplished and very beautiful feel one experiences in the genteel Boston impressionists, particularly Edmund Charles Tarbell. At their best, these works have a lustrous radiance animated by the diffuse, filtered light penetrating her simple spatial divisions. During the 1920s, however, her compositions began to dissolve into ambiguous abstractions, even as she continued to depict group scenes of mothers and children. In these paintings, limbs taper off into unresolved points, mere brush strokes. In 1926, Wiley suffered a breakdown and was hospitalized for the rest of her life. One can almost imagine this very late work as providing the same evidence of disintegrating mental health one experiences in late work by Van Gogh. Note that the entire work is an exercise in the application of paint, resulting in a highly abstract image in which one can barely distinguish representational form. As such, it is a sad but fascinating document of a deeply talented artist on the edge of total collapse.

PROVENANCE
John Coker Antiques, New Market, Tennessee; by purchase to Southeastern Newspapers Corporation; by gift to Morris Museum of Art.

LITERATURE
Keyes, Donald. *Impressionism and the South.* Greenville County Museum of Art, Greenville, South Carolina, 1988.

Layman, Earl D. *The Paintings of Miss Catherine Wiley.* The Dulin Gallery of Art, Knoxville, Tennessee, 1964.

Moffat, Frederick C. "Painting, Sculpture and Photography." *Heart of the Valley.* Knoxville, Tennessee, 1976.

Pennington, Estill Curtis. "Catherine Wiley: Genteel Southern Impressionist." *Southern Impressionist: The Art of Catherine Wiley.* Tennessee State Museum, Knoxville, 1990.

ARCHIVAL SOURCES
Tennessee State Museum, curatorial files, Knoxville.

## LOUIS L. BETTS

1873-1961

Born, Little Rock, Arkansas; studied with his father, the painter Edwin Daniel Betts, Sr., and at the Pennsylvania Academy of Design with William Merritt Chase, 1901; intermittent activity in the Mississippi River Valley; died, New York City.

### The Yellow Parasol

c. 1925, signed lower left
Oil on canvas, 50 x 40 inches
1991.003

Betts was a member of a large family of artists who often returned to the South on painting expeditions from Chicago. His brother, H.H. Betts, is known to have painted in Natchez and Vicksburg, and Betts, himself, was a frequent visitor to Arkansas. While the subject matter of ladies in historical dress sporting parasols is not restricted to the South, the date and style of the painting are manifestations of certain retardataire trends in the Southern impressionist art of the period. Curiously enough, Betts' figures wear the romantic garb of the Colonial Revival, floating, dreamlike, through an imaginary garden, even as the noise of jazz-age cubism was nearly deafening. This work apparently was part of a series of works painted by Betts during the 1920s at Old Lyme, Connecticut, a colony of artists working in the impressionist manner under the influence and patronage of Florence Griswold.

#### PROVENANCE
From the estate of the artist to Sarah Gardner Betts, his widow; sold at Sotheby Parke Bernet, New York, January 30, 1980, number 292; private collection, Connecticut; to Daniel B. Grossman, Inc., Fine Art, New York; by purchase to Southeastern Newspapers Corporation; by gift to Morris Museum of Art.

#### LITERATURE
Clark, Eliot. *History of the National Academy of Design, 1825-1953.* New York City, 1954.

Earle, Helen L. *Biographical Sketches of American Artists.* Michigan State Library, Lansing, 1924.

Gerdts, William H. *Art Across America: Two Centuries of Regional Painting, 1720-1920.* New York City, 1990.

Hackley Art Gallery, Muskegon, Michigan. "Louis Betts." *Aesthetics* 2, no. 3 (April 1914).

Mayor, A. Hyatt and David Mark. *American Art at the Century.* The Century Association, New York City, 1977.

#### ARCHIVAL SOURCES
Smithsonian Institution Fine Arts Library, artist's files.

#### EXHIBITION HISTORY
This work appears, by verisimilitude of detail, to be the same work exhibited as *Summer* at the National Academy of Design in 1925, where it won the Obrig Prize. (*Art World* magazine, August 11, 1925.)

HATTIE SAUSSY

1890-1978

Born, Savannah, Georgia; studied in Savannah with Emma Cheves Wilkins, at the New York School of Fine and Applied Art, and at the Art Students League with Eugene Speicher and Frank Vincent Dumond, 1912; active in Savannah, north Georgia, and the Carolinas throughout her life, and in New Orleans 1947-1952; died, Savannah.

*In the Hall*

c. 1925, signed lower right
Oil on academy board, 20 x 24 inches
1989.01.172

Saussy's art was well-grounded in the local Savannah arts traditions fostered by Lila Cabaniss and Emma Cheves Wilkins, a tradition that produced several outstanding women artists in the same period. Her subsequent work with Frank Vincent Dumond at the Art Students League in New York ensured a mature style that combined the color fields of international impressionism with the rather brushy naturalism of the American school. Of independent means, Miss Saussy painted for her own pleasure, a pursuit that she followed diligently, nevertheless. A deeply religious person, Saussy was inspired by nature as a spiritual conduit to a deeper awareness she expressed through her art. According to Thetis Rush, her "paintings were not done for the purpose of instructing or appealing ... to an artistic intelligentsia (but) with the hope that her work would stir a feeling in her viewer akin to her own" (p. 4).

**PROVENANCE**
From the artist by gift to Myrtle Jones, Savannah, Georgia; to Terry H. Lowenthal, Savannah; by purchase to Robert Powell Coggins Collection; by purchase to Southeastern Newspapers Corporation; by gift to Morris Museum of Art.

**LITERATURE**
Chambers, Bruce. *Art and Artists of the South.* Columbia, South Carolina, 1984.

Kelly, James C. *The South on Paper.* Spartanburg, South Carolina, 1985.

Rush, Thetis. *Hattie Saussy: Georgia Painter.* Spartanburg, South Carolina, 1983.

**ARCHIVAL SOURCES**
Archives of American Art, Smithsonian Institution.

Georgia Historical Society, Savannah, Georgia.

**EXHIBITION HISTORY**
Southern States Art League, 7th Annual Exhibition, Gibbes Art Gallery, Charleston, South Carolina, 1927; "Exhibition of Georgia Art," Davison-Paxton Company, Atlanta, January 16-25, 1928; "Women in Art: Early Twentieth Century Collections from the Collection of Robert P. Coggins, M.D.," Arnold Gallery, Shorter College, Rome, Georgia, November 16-25, 1980; "Art and Artists of the South: The Robert Powell Coggins Collection," 1984-1986. (See note on catalog organization for complete exhibition schedule.)

# WILLIAM WOODWARD

1859-1939

Born, Seekonk, Massachusetts; studied, Rhode Island School of Design, 1877-1883, and at the Academie Julien, Paris, France 1886; active in New Orleans, 1885-1923; died, Biloxi, Mississippi.

## *View Toward Old Bain Street*

c. 1925, signed lower left
Oil crayon on academy board, 14¾ x 19 inches
1989.05.271

In 1921 William Woodward was severely injured in a fall from a scaffold while painting a mural in the lobby of the United Fruit Company in New Orleans. After that, he retired from teaching and lived for most of the year at a home on the Gulf Coast of Mississippi near Biloxi. However, he continued to paint, re-creating many of his earlier works documenting the architectural heritage of the French Quarter. He was motivated by a fear that the French Quarter, which at the turn of the century was a neglected Bohemian slum, might disappear.

This work is a variant of *Toulouse Street at Bourbon* painted in 1904 and published as number 5 in the Byrnes volume. The viewer stands with his back downriver looking toward the Old Basin, which connected Lake Pontchartrain and Bayou St. John and acted as a docking point for vessels carrying commodities and produce to the inner city. The Byrneses admired the artist's efforts: "Woodward emerges as an objective observer who, despite a dedication to realism, managed to infuse a gentle romanticism through a sensitive rendition of the special light and atmosphere characteristic of the Old World City."

### PROVENANCE
From the artist to Carl Woodward; to Downtown Gallery, New Orleans; by purchase to Southeastern Newspapers Corporation; by gift to Morris Museum of Art.

### LITERATURE
Byrnes, Barbara and James. *Early Views of the Vieux Carré*. New Orleans, 1965.

Cullison, William R., III. *Two Southern Impressionists: An Exhibition of the Work of the Woodward Brothers, William and Ellsworth*. Art Collection of Tulane University, New Orleans, 1984.

Heidelberg, Michelle Favrot. *William Woodward*. Unpublished master's thesis, Tulane University, New Orleans, 1974.

Keyes, Donald. *Impressionism and the South*. Greenville County Museum of Art, Greenville, South Carolina, 1988.

Mahe, John A., II and Rosanne McCaffrey. *Encyclopedia of New Orleans Artists 1718-1918*. Historic New Orleans Collection, New Orleans, 1987.

Ormond, Suzanne and Mary E. Irvine. *Louisiana's Art Nouveau: The Crafts of the Newcomb Style*. Gretna, Louisiana, 1976.

Pennington, Estill Curtis. *Downriver: Currents of Style in Louisiana Painting 1801-1950*. Gretna, Louisiana, 1991.

Poesch, Jessie. *Newcomb Pottery: An Enterprise for Southern Women, 1895-1940*. Exton, Pennsylvania, 1984.

Virginia Museum. *Painting in the South: 1564-1980*. Richmond, 1983.

Woodward, William. *French Quarter Etchings of Old New Orleans*. New Orleans, 1938.

### ARCHIVAL SOURCES
Historic New Orleans Collection, artist's files.

Howard-Tilton Memorial Library, Special Collections and Louisiana Collection, Tulane University, New Orleans.

## WILLIAM POSEY SILVA

1859-1948

Born, Savannah, Georgia; studied with Arthur Wesley Dow at Ipswich, Massachusetts, summers, 1900-1906, and at the Academie Julien, Paris, France 1907; active in Chattanooga, Tennessee, 1887-1910, in Washington, D.C., 1910-1913, and intermittently in Georgia, South Carolina, Louisiana, Texas, and Mississippi, 1913-1948; died, Carmel-by-the-Sea, California.

### *Raiment of Springtime*

1931, signed and dated lower right
Oil on canvas, 10⅛ x 24 inches
1989.01.185

Although he had pursued painting as a hobby, Silva became a professional artist quite late in life, when at the age of 48 he sold his business in Chattanooga and moved to Paris, where he enrolled in the Academie Julien. Upon his return to this country, he traveled throughout the South with the vigor of an itinerant portrait artist in search of landscape subject matter. Always the coastal regions of Carolina and Mississippi appealed to him. This work is more than likely from a series of paintings Silva based on his study of Middleton Gardens outside of Charleston. He was captivated by the shimmering quality of the humid light dancing on the vegetation and the close color harmonics of the ancient garden, which he painted many times.

**PROVENANCE**
From Dave Knoke Gallery, Atlanta, to Robert Powell Coggins Collection; by purchase to Southeastern Newspapers Corporation; by gift to Morris Museum of Art.

**LITERATURE**
Chambers, Bruce. *Art and Artists of the South.* Columbia, South Carolina, 1984.

Kelly, James C. "Landscape and Genre Painting in Tennessee, 1810-1985." *Tennessee State Historical Quarterly* 44, no. 2 (Summer 1985).

Keyes, Donald. *Impressionism and the South.* Greenville County Museum of Art, Greenville, South Carolina, 1988.

Mechlin, Leila. "William Posey Silva – An Appreciation." *The American Magazine of Art* (January 1923).

Virginia Museum. *Painting in the South: 1564-1980.* Richmond, 1983.

**ARCHIVAL SOURCES**
Archives of American Art, Smithsonian Institution.

Smithsonian Institution Fine Arts Library, artist's files.

# CLARENCE MILLET

1897-1959

Born, Hahnville, Louisiana; studied with Louis O. Griffith and Robert Grafton in New Orleans, 1916; and at the Art Students League in New York City, 1922-1924; active in New Orleans throughout his career; died, New Orleans.

## *The Prudhomme-Rouquier House, Natchitoches*

1941, signed lower right
Oil on canvas, 31 x 36 inches
1992.029

The Prudhomme-Rouquier House in Natchitoches, Louisiana, is one of the oldest surviving bousillage-type houses. Bousillage is an interior wall-filler, composed of mud reinforced with Spanish moss and deer hair, a compound that was spread between cypress frames, ensuring a cool, well-insulated interior. The core of the house was built by Francois Rouquier, a wealthy landowner from North Carolina, and his wife, Marie Louise Prudhomme, daughter of Jean Baptiste Prudhomme, a figure of note in the early history of northern Louisiana. This core was built before 1800. After 1811, when the house was acquired by the Carr family, it was extensively remodeled and given the spanning gallery in the classical idiom, which can be seen in Millet's painting.

Millet is known to have visited the house several times during the 1930s. At that time, he worked in his own style of impressionism, coloring in cool tones and using mauves and grays to create a highly romantic sense of place, a place more often lit by the reflective glow of an imaginary moon rather than the more demanding, unrelenting light of the sun at full semi-tropical peak. This gives the work a symbolic, as well as a representational, character, evoking the spirit of nostalgia even as it documents survival. Such is often the case in the South.

### PROVENANCE
Painted for Mr. and Mrs. Wesley Cocram as a wedding gift; acquired from Mrs. L.D. Allen (the former Mrs. Cocram) for the Roger Houston Ogden Collection, New Orleans; by exchange to the Morris Museum of Art.

### LITERATURE
Anglo-American Art Museum. *The Louisiana Landscape 1800-1969.* Baton Rouge, Louisiana, 1969.

Louisiana State University. *Louisiana Artists from the Collection of Dr. and Mrs. James W. Nelson.* Baton Rouge, 1968.

Pennington, Estill Curtis. *Downriver: Currents of Style in Louisiana Painting 1800-1950.* Gretna, Louisiana, 1991.

### ARCHIVAL SOURCES
Historic New Orleans Collection, artist's files.

Works Progress Administration Papers, New Orleans Museum of Art.

Howard-Tilton Memorial Library, Special Collections and Louisiana Collection, Tulane University, New Orleans.

### EXHIBITION HISTORY
"Louisiana Art from the Ogden Collection," Louisiana State Archives Building, Baton Rouge, March 6-April 16, 1988.

## ANTHONY THIEME

1888-1954

Born, Rotterdam, Holland; studied at the Academy of Fine Arts, Rotterdam, and the Royal Academy, The Hague; active in Charleston, South Carolina, and St. Augustine, Florida, 1946-1948; died, New York.

### *Charleston Doorway*

c. 1946, signed lower left
Oil on canvas, 30½ x 36½ inches
1989.01.205

Thieme appeared in the South very late in his career. In the aftermath of a disastrous fire at his studio in Cape Ann near Rockport, Massachusetts, he traveled to Charleston in search of new subject matter. Prior to that time his specialty had been New England coastal scenes of a rather illustrative nature, in a muted palette of limited range. Once in Charleston, however, as Bruce Chambers notes, the "serenity and tonal discipline of his seascapes was abandoned for the elaborations of wrought iron and profusion of blossoms that Charleston imposed on his senses" (p. 81). No subject could have been more typical than the doorway with lunette fanlight he depicts. With the vibrant colors of the flowers and the warmth and glow of a strong semi-tropical light, the painting is at once a simple architectural essay and a symbolic evocation of Southern hospitality.

#### PROVENANCE
From Elizabeth Grover Johnson by gift to Memorial Art Gallery of the University of Rochester, 1975; deaccessed, 1978; by purchase to Robert Powell Coggins Collection; by purchase to Southeastern Newspapers Corporation; by gift to Morris Museum of Art.

#### LITERATURE
Chambers, Bruce. *Art and Artists of the South.* Columbia, South Carolina, 1984.

#### ARCHIVAL SOURCES
Grand Central Gallery, artist's files, New York City.

Memorial Art Gallery of the University of Rochester, artist's files, Rochester, New York.

Smithsonian Institution Fine Arts Library, artist's files.

#### EXHIBITION HISTORY
Grand Central Gallery, New York City, 1947 (?); "Art and Artists of the South: The Robert Powell Coggins Collection," 1984-1986. (See note on catalog organization for complete exhibition schedule.)

A J Drysdale
1916

# Works on Paper

Works on paper are art objects created in a wide range of finish, from rough sketches to finely executed drawings and watercolors. In almost every instance, the creative impetus for these works is more spontaneous, and, indeed, more site-specific, than one associates with a painting. A painting is quite often a studio product, and likely to have been created from the work on paper.

Once completed, a painting often takes on a slightly mystical aura, which removes it from the more obvious thematic concerns of locale. With this in mind, it is possible to see works on paper as documents, recording the artist's sensate response to locale, rendered in a particular style or format.

Most of the works in this section were created in the critical hundred-year span from 1860 to 1960. During that time, the South moved from a restrictive, agrarian economy, sustained by slave labor, through war and upheaval, toward reconciliation and the mainstream of American life. Along that route, Southern artists were observing with critical, humorous, colorful, and insightful eye. One would like to think they sought, even as they worked, to evoke a sense of time and place that, though now vanished, lingers delicately in the mind's eye, on the paper at hand.

JOHN ABBOT

1751-1840

Born, London, England; studied with Jacob Bonneau; immigrated to America in 1773; active in Virginia 1773-1775, in Burke County, Georgia, 1776-1818, and in Bulloch County, Georgia, 1813-1840; died in Bulloch County.

*Pale Yellow Throat*

1790
Watercolor on hand-laid paper
11⅛ x 8¾ inches
1981.B-003

John Abbot's art is part of that body of work drawn by late eighteenth- and early nineteenth-century naturalists reflecting the Anglo-American passion to seek, describe and catalog the living creatures of this virgin wilderness. Vivian Rogers-Price and William Griffin give Abbot considerable credit for his role in establishing American ornithology: "Abbot's equally important contributions to ornithology were realized through his friendship with Alexander Wilson, the father of American ornithology, whom Abbot met in 1809 in Savannah. Abbot freely shared his nearly forty years of study in America with Wilson and George Ord (1781-1866), the American naturalist who completed the last two volumes of American Ornithology (1808-1814) following Wilson's death in 1813."

Rogers-Price and Griffin note that while Wilson is given credit for discovering several new species of birds in the Southeast, their discovery, description and habits were a credit to Abbot. "Significantly (these new species) which Abbot knew, collected and illustrated prior to publication of their descriptions, were nondescript birds easily overlooked or confused with other species except by an astute observer." Abbot's gentle, colorful watercolors reflect that well-attuned eye that led to such discoveries, as well as the discipline of a profound and complex creative imagination.

PROVENANCE
Purchased in London from the Ibarcord Group, S.A., through the offices of Andrew Crawley, to the collection of Southeastern Newspapers Corporation; by gift to Morris Museum of Art.

LITERATURE
Coulbourn, Keith. "Life and Times of John Abbot, Naturalist." *Atlanta Journal and Constitution* magazine, April 29, 1973.

Kelly, James C. *The South on Paper*. Spartanburg, South Carolina, 1985.

Remington, C.L. "John Abbot: Notes on My Life." *Lepidopterists' News* 2 (March 1948).

Rogers-Price, Vivian and William W. Griffin. "John Abbot: Pioneer-Naturalist of Georgia." *Antiques* (October 1983).

Rogers-Price, Vivian. *John Abbot in Georgia: The Vision of a Naturalist Artist (1751-ca.1840)*. Madison, Georgia, 1983.

ARCHIVAL SOURCES
Museum of Comparative Zoology, Harvard University, Cambridge, Massachusetts.

University of Georgia Libraries, Special Collections Division, Athens.

65.

## (MR.) BARNARD (BERNARD)

Possibly the artist Anna Wells Rutledge identifies as painting a series of landscape works in Charleston in 1831, and about whom nothing else is known.

### *Apollo and the Muses*

1829
Graphite on paper, 19⅞ x 27⅜ inches
Robert Powell Coggins Art Trust,
Morris Museum of Art COG-1494

At best, a tentative link may exist between the artist of "three successive 'Views of Charleston' from the harbor … by … Mr. Bernard …" and the artist of this work. The proximity of Charleston and Savannah, and the awkward rendering and simple sense of line in both works account for the attribution, put forth bravely, at best. The drawing itself is a copy of a well-known work of the late eighteenth century, *Parnassus*, by Raphael Mengs, which adorned the ceiling of Cardinal Albani's apartment in Rome. Kenneth Clark, in *The Romantic Rebellion*, refers to the fresco as "insipid … fundamentally frivolous. It does not reflect life, but some vapid dream of connoisseurs and collectors." Clark's flagging admiration aside, it was engraved and became a cornerstone of neo-classical design, especially when used as a print source for drawing classes. It is of importance here as an example of a provincial artist drawing upon outside sources and demonstrating to a local audience certain mainstreams of international ambition.

**PROVENANCE**
Source unknown; discovered in the Robert Powell Coggins Collection; to Robert Powell Coggins Art Trust, Morris Museum of Art.

**LITERATURE**
Rutledge, Anna Wells. *Artists in the Life of Charleston.* Columbia, South Carolina, 1980.

# HELEN TURNER

1858-1958

Born, Louisville, Kentucky; studied, Artists Association of New Orleans, with Bror Wikstrom and Andres Molinary, 1886-1893, and at the Art Students League with Kenyon Cox and William Merritt Chase, 1895-1899; active in New Orleans, 1880-1893 and 1926-1949; died, New Orleans.

## *A Country Road*

c. 1893, signed lower right
Graphite on paper, 10⅞ x 17 inches
1989.05.266

The strong foreground and flagrant exploitation of vanishing perspective apparent in this work are obvious manifestations of Helen Turner's period of study with Andres Molinary and the artists of the Louisiana landscape school. In that tradition, she leads the eye from frontal confrontation to an ambiguous distant point, drawing the viewer ever deeper into a monochromatic world, enhanced by the shadings of gray and white.

### PROVENANCE
From the artist's estate; in passing; to Keith Marshall, Madewood Plantation, New Orleans; by purchase to Southeastern Newspapers Corporation; by gift to Morris Museum of Art.

### LITERATURE
Keyes, Donald. *Impressionism in the South.* Greenville County Museum of Art, Greenville, South Carolina, 1988.

Mahe, John A., II and Rosanne McCaffrey. *Encyclopedia of New Orleans Artists 1718-1918.* Historic New Orleans Collection, New Orleans, 1987.

Mount, May W. *Some Notables of New Orleans: Biographical and Descriptive Sketches of the Artists of New Orleans and their work.* New Orleans, 1987.

Rabbage, L.H. *Helen M. Turner, N.A. (1858-1958).* Cragsmoor Free Library, Cragsmoor, New York, 1983.

### ARCHIVAL SOURCES
Cragsmoor Free Library, Cragsmoor, New York.

Historic New Orleans Collection, artist's files.

### EXHIBITION HISTORY
"A Sense of Time and Place: Works on Paper from the Morris Museum of Art," Greenville County Museum of Art, Greenville, South Carolina, March 5-April 21, 1991.

## ALICE RAVENEL HUGER SMITH

1876-1958

Born, and died, Charleston, South Carolina, where she was active as an artist throughout her life.

### *Lowland Waterway by the Moonlight*

1915, signed and dated lower right
Watercolor on paper, 26½ x 18 inches
Robert Powell Coggins Art Trust,
Morris Museum of Art COG-8004

In an age in which the term "self-taught" has taken on such definitive meaning, it is ironic to note that Smith was largely a self-taught artist. Though her visionary instinct did not draw her into those curiously disjunctured personal expressions the term currently connotes, her singular vision of the Carolina low country is no less perceptive. Martha Severens, in material prepared for an exhibition of the artist's work at the Gibbes Gallery in Charleston in 1984, makes an important historical notation on her sources: "As an artist Alice Smith was deeply influenced by Japanese prints of the Ukiyo-e school. Her friend, Motte Alston Read, assembled a collection of these prints which she both studied and catalogued. Like the Oriental artist, Alice Smith regarded nature's beauties reverently and captured their fleeting quality. Her compositions, likewise, are frequently asymmetrical and understated, enhancing the gentle poetry of the landscape."

In this work there is that same spare, Japanese quality of design, enlightened by Smith's special understanding of the emanative quality of light, which seeps through the scene with a cutting edge dividing space and form, animating the distance, raising the mystery of the isolated setting to a transcendental level.

#### PROVENANCE
Robert M. Hicklin, Jr., Inc., Spartanburg, South Carolina; to Robert Powell Coggins Collection; to Robert Powell Coggins Art Trust, Morris Museum of Art.

#### LITERATURE
*Alice Ravenel Huger Smith: An Appreciation on the Occasion of Her Eightieth Birthday, from her Friends.* Charleston, South Carolina, 1956.

Chambers, Bruce. *Art and Artists of the South.* Columbia, South Carolina, 1984.

Severens, Martha. "Lady of the Low Country." *South Carolina Wildlife* (March-April 1979).

. "Reveries: The Work of Alice Ravenel Huger Smith." *Art Voices South 1* (January-February 1978).

Smith, Alice Ravenel Huger. *A Charleston Sketchbook 1796-1806, Forty Watercolor Drawings of the City and the Surrounding Country, Including Plantations and Parish Churches.* Carolina Art Association, Charleston, South Carolina, 1940.

Smith, D.E. Huger. *A Charlestonian's Recollections 1846-1913.* Charleston, South Carolina, 1950.

Smith, D.E. Huger and Alice Ravenel Huger Smith. *A Carolina Rice Plantation of the Fifties.* New York City, 1936.

. *Charles Fraser.* Charleston, South Carolina, 1924.

. *The Dwelling Houses of Charleston.* Charleston, South Carolina, 1917.

Virginia Museum. *Painting in the South: 1564-1980.* Richmond, 1983.

#### ARCHIVAL SOURCES
Gibbes Art Gallery, artist's files, Charleston, South Carolina.

South Carolina Historical Society, Charleston.

#### EXHIBITION HISTORY
"A Sense of Time and Place: Works on Paper from the Morris Museum of Art," Greenville County Museum of Art, Greenville, South Carolina, March 5-April 21, 1991.

## ALEXANDER JOHN DRYSDALE

1870-1934

Born, Marietta, Georgia; studied with Paul Poincy at the Southern Art Union, New Orleans, 1887, and with Frank Vincent Dumond at the Art Students League, New York, 1901-1903; active in New Orleans, 1903-1934; died, New Orleans.

### *Bayou Landscape*

1916, signed and dated lower left
Thinned oil on board, 20¼ x 30¼ inches
Robert Powell Coggins Art Trust,
Morris Museum of Art COG-0352

Several spurious myths attend Drysdale's life and art, not the least of which are rumors of profligacy and alcoholism. Much effort has been expended by historians, particularly Dr. Buechner, to dispel those rumors. Drysdale was actually a very productive artist, whose somewhat endless repetition of certain formulaic compositions in his landscape art has caused his efforts to be undervalued.

Drysdale's medium was his most idiosyncratic invention. By diluting oil paint with kerosene, he created a very fluid wash. This was applied to the surface of the work with brush and cotton balls. While giving the work a very aqueous feel, it also is rife with inherent vice, with the result that many of his paintings on artist board now have glowing rings around the naturalistic elements.

Composition in Drysdale's art is always a variation on the theme of vanishing perspective, offset by the placement of a strongly defined tree in the foreground. Set either right or left of center, it heralds a meandering stream moving into the picture plane to a distant background point. This work has a more lucent presence than many. A rather vibrant intensity in the lilies in the foreground works to strengthen the depth and distance of the work, further compounded by the vaporous blue-green glow of the shadowy trees in the distant background. Note the undulating interplay between the strongly defined naturalistic forms on the left and the diaphanous forms on the right, linked by the curving line of the bayou waterway.

#### PROVENANCE
From Sammy J. Hardeman, Atlanta; to Robert Powell Coggins Collection; to Robert Powell Coggins Art Trust, Morris Museum of Art.

#### LITERATURE
Anglo-American Art Museum. *The Louisiana Landscape 1800-1969.* Baton Rouge, Louisiana, 1969.

Buechner, Howard A. *Drysdale (1870-1934): Artist of Myth and Legend.* Metairie, Louisiana, 1985.

Chambers, Bruce. *Art and Artists of the South.* Columbia, South Carolina, 1984.

Cline, Isaac Monroe. *Contemporary Art and Artists in New Orleans.* Louisiana State Museum, New Orleans, 1924.

Kelly, James C. *The South on Paper.* Spartanburg, South Carolina, 1985.

Mahe, John A., II and Rosanne McCaffrey. *Encyclopedia of New Orleans Artists 1718-1918.* Historic New Orleans Collection, New Orleans, 1987.

Pennington, Estill Curtis. *Downriver: Currents of Style in Louisiana Painting 1800-1950.* Gretna, Louisiana, 1991.

——. *Look Away: Reality and Sentiment in Southern Art.* Atlanta, 1989.

Virginia Museum. *Painting in the South: 1564-1980.* Richmond, 1983.

Wiesendanger, Martin and Margaret Wiesendanger. *19th Century Painters and Paintings from the Collection of W.E. Groves.* Gretna, Louisiana, 1971.

#### ARCHIVAL SOURCES
Historic New Orleans Collection, artist's files.

Howard-Tilton Memorial Library, Louisiana Collection, Tulane University, New Orleans.

#### EXHIBITION HISTORY
"A Sense of Time and Place: Works on Paper from the Morris Museum of Art," Greenville County Museum of Art, Greenville, South Carolina, March 5-April 21, 1991.

## GARI MELCHERS

1860-1932

Born, Detroit; studied, Royal Academy at Dusseldorf, 1877-1883, and at the Ecole des Beaux Arts, Paris, France, 1883-1884; active in Fredericksburg, Virginia, 1916-1932; died, Fredericksburg. (?)

### Sketch of Young Black Woman in White Dress and Hat

c. 1925, signed lower right
Oil on paper, 18½ x 11 inches
1989.01.117

Melchers' marriage in 1903 to Corinne Lawton Mackall of Savannah gave his life a permanent Southern exposure in the years that followed. After the advent of the First World War, the Melcherses moved back to America in 1915 and established residency at an eighteenth-century house, Belmont, outside Fredericksburg, Virginia. Thereafter, Melchers applied the same strongly academic approach to Southern subject matter that he had used earlier in his period in Holland when he created monumental works in a brightly colored Dutch genre mode.

While *The Hunters* is the most notable of his Southern works, it is interesting to note that he also painted several black subjects. In 1925, during an automobile trip to Savannah from Virginia, Melchers stopped in Adam's Run, South Carolina, where he painted a schoolroom scene in gouache. Coloration and compositional format would seem to link this work to that sketching trip. Melchers' grasp of the verve and vitality of his subject, together with his smashing palette, makes this one of his finest surviving sketches.

**PROVENANCE**
Christie's East sale; to Robert Powell Coggins Collection; by purchase to Southeastern Newspapers Corporation; by gift to Morris Museum of Art.

**LITERATURE**
Donaldson, Bruce M. *Gari Melchers: A Memorial Exhibition of His Work.* Virginia Museum, Richmond, 1938.

Lesko, Diane and Esther Persson, et. al. *Gari Melchers.* St. Petersburg, Florida, 1990. (Includes the definitive bibliography to date, as well as essays by George Mesman, Annette Scott, Jennifer Bienenstock, Joseph Dreiss, Feay Coleman, Richard Reid, Ronald Van Vleuten, and Joanna Catron on a wide range of issues connected with Melchers' life and career.)

Orseman, Janice C. *Gari Melchers 1860-1932: American Painter.* Graham Gallery, New York, 1978.

Reid, Richard S. "Gari Melchers: An American Artist in Virginia." *Virginia Cavalcade* 28 (Spring 1979).

Virginia Museum. *Painting in the South: 1564-1980.* Richmond, 1983.

**ARCHIVAL SOURCES**
Archives of American Art, Smithsonian Institution.

Belmont, The Gari Melchers Memorial Gallery, Fredericksburg, Virginia.

Smithsonian Institution Fine Arts Library, artist's files.

**EXHIBITION HISTORY**
"'Art and Artists of the South' and Recent Acquisitions," Georgia Museum of Art, University of Georgia, Athens, January 9-February 21, 1988; "A Sense of Time and Place: Works on Paper from the Morris Museum of Art," Greenville County Museum of Art, Greenville, South Carolina, March 5-April 21, 1991.

ALFRED HUTTY

1877-1954

Born, Grand Haven, Michigan; studied at Art Students League Summer School in Woodstock, New York, with Birge Harrison, 1907; active in Charleston, South Carolina, 1919-1954; died, Woodstock.

*Hanging Clothes*

c. 1925
Watercolor and graphite on paper
24⅞ x 20¾ inches
Robert Powell Coggins Art Trust,
Morris Museum of Art COG-1198

Hutty's oft-quoted remark to his wife regarding Charleston: "Come quick; have found paradise," should have a dual meaning. In Hutty's art, Charleston becomes a paradise, and it was largely through his inspiration that the arts community of the crumbling city was revitalized, sparking a profound renaissance. Though known primarily as an etcher and engraver, Hutty was adept in several media. The few surviving oils from his Charleston period are impressionistic essays on the dramatic color of the local scene. His smaller drawings and watercolors, many of which served as foundations for his prints, are far more perceptive observations on the local scene. *Hanging Clothes* displays two of Hutty's best recurring compositional devices. His abilities as a draftsman are more than apparent in the well-defined rounded lines of his standing figures. At the same time, the teasing play of line created by the wavering clothesline gives the work a restless energy of great charm.

**PROVENANCE**
Ray Holsclaw, Charleston, South Carolina; to Robert Powell Coggins Collection; to Robert Powell Coggins Art Trust, Morris Museum of Art.

**LITERATURE**
Chambers, Bruce. *Art and Artists of the South.* Columbia, South Carolina, 1984.

Gibbes Art Gallery. *Alfred Hutty: A Memorial Exhibition.* Carolina Art Association, Charleston, South Carolina, 1956.

Harrison, Birge. "Old Charleston As Pictured by Alfred Hutty." *The American Magazine of Art,* 192?.

Kelly, James C. *The South on Paper.* Spartanburg, South Carolina, 1985.

Phillips, Duncan. "Alfred Hutty." *American Etchers,* Vol. II, New York, 1929.

Saunders, Boyd and Ann McAden. *Alfred Hutty and the Charleston Renaissance.* Orangeburg, South Carolina, 1990.

**ARCHIVAL SOURCES**
Archives of American Art, Smithsonian Institution.

Gibbes Art Gallery, artist's files, Charleston, South Carolina.

ELIZABETH WHITE

1883-1976

Born, Sumter, South Carolina; studied with Wayman Adams at the Pennsylvania Academy of Fine Arts; active in Charleston and Sumter throughout her life, died, Sumter.

*Woodland Idyll, Brookgreen Gardens*

1928, signed lower left
Pastel on paper, 16½ x 11½ inches
1990.091

White's evanescent pastels are an inspired reminder of the power of the late impressionist technique to capture the atmosphere and mystery of a remote deep South landscape. As a native of Sumter, South Carolina, she often drew upon local scenes for her work in a variety of media. As a follower of Alfred Hutty and the artists of the Charleston Renaissance, she was well versed in the application of color laid down in close value. Notice in this work the deftly controlled modulations between shadings of lavender and live oak green, relieved by occasional highlights in red.

PROVENANCE:
From J. Petty, to the Robert Powell Coggins Collection; by purchase to Southeastern Newspapers Corporation; by gift to the Morris Museum of Art.

LITERATURE
Parris, Nina. *South Carolina Collection 1770-1985*, The Columbia Museum. Columbia, South Carolina.

Eaves, James M., ed. *Memoranda on the Life and Work of Ms. Elizabeth White*. Unpublished manuscript, Sumter, South Carolina, 1986.

Greenville County Museum of Art. *Work Song*. Greenville, South Carolina, 1990.

ARCHIVAL SOURCES
Center for the Study of Southern Painting, Morris Museum of Art.

Smithsonian Institution Fine Arts Library, artist's files.

EXHIBITION HISTORY
Possibly the work exhibited in a retrospective show in Columbia in 1957 and listed as No. 3, "Woodland Idyll, Brookgreen Gardens"; "A Sense of Time and Place: Works on Paper from the Morris Museum of Art," Greenville County Museum of Art, Greenville, South Carolina, March 5-April 21, 1991.

WILL HENRY STEVENS

1881-1949

Born, Vevay, Indiana; studied at the Cincinnati Art Academy, 1901-1904; active in New Orleans and in Asheville, North Carolina, 1920-1949; died, New Orleans.

*Cubist Mountain View*

c. 1935, signed lower right
Mixed media on paper, 20¾ x 19¼ inches
Robert Powell Coggins Art Trust,
Morris Museum of Art  COG-0244

Throughout the 1930s, Stevens' painting style began to evolve into non-objective forms. A review of the growth of his art in this period reveals that he was not spontaneously avant-garde. Like Cezanne, his art begins to break form down into interacting fields of color.  Indeed, it is possible to see his work as a form of analytic cubism in the spirit of Braque and the early Picasso. The mature style that emerges from Stevens' brush during his most original period is very similar to that of Kandinsky, Klee, and Arshile Gorky. Those paintings are often described as lyrical. Art critic W.M. Darling, reviewing an exhibition of Stevens' work at the Arts and Crafts Club in New Orleans for the *Times-Picayune* in 1945, thought them to be "paintings in which not one false note, one error in relationship, asserts itself ... absolute harmony prevails."

Harmonic is an accurate description for Stevens' color values. Though he was obviously concerned with the psychological implications of non-objective painting, his own work depends upon an interrelationship of color values rather than jarring juxtapositions, well planned, rather than spontaneous, and subtle rather than arresting. His interacting forms, though abstract, are devoid of the undercurrent of disturbance that characterizes so much of the art of his period. This sensational transitional work clearly illustrates Stevens' movement from the representational to the abstract. Echoes of Cezanne abound in the shadows of the background mountain range. Even so, key Stevens motifs, particularly in the amorphous blobs of turquoise and russet, are beginning to appear.

**PROVENANCE**
From the estate of the artist to New Morning Gallery, Asheville, North Carolina; by purchase to Robert Powell Coggins Collection; to Robert Powell Coggins Art Trust, Morris Museum of Art.

**LITERATURE**
Kelly, James C. *The South on Paper.* Spartanburg, South Carolina, 1985.

Lehman, Bernard. *Will Henry's Nature: The Pictorial Ideas of W.H. Stevens.* Unpublished manuscript, 1947-1948. Tulane University Archives, New Orleans.

North, Percy. "Nature's Spirit in the Abstractions of Will Henry Stevens." *SECAC Review* (1989).

——. *Visions of an Inner Life, Abstractions by Will Henry Stevens.* Emory University Museum of Art and Archaeology, Atlanta, 1988.

Pennington, Estill Curtis. *Downriver: Currents of Style in Louisiana Painting 1800-1950.* Gretna, Louisiana, 1991.

Poesch, Jessie. *Will Henry Stevens.* Greenville County Museum of Art, Greenville, South Carolina, 1987. (Contains the definitive bibliography to date.)

——. "Will Henry Stevens…Modern Mystic: Beginnings to 1921." *The Southern Quarterly* 25, no. 1 (Fall 1986).

Virginia Museum. *Painting in the South: 1564-1980.* Richmond, 1983.

York, Richard T. *Will Henry Stevens (1881-1949): A Modernist's Response to Nature.* Richard York Gallery, New York, 1987.

**ARCHIVAL SOURCES**
Historic New Orleans Collection, artist's files.

Howard-Tilton Memorial Library, Special Collections and Louisiana Collection, Tulane University, New Orleans.

Indianapolis Museum of Art archives.

McDowell Collection, Stevens family archives, Asheville, North Carolina.

New Orleans Museum of Art, curatorial files.

# WALTER ANDERSON

1903-1965

Born, New Orleans; studied at the Pennsylvania Academy of Fine Arts; 1924-1929; active, Ocean Springs, Mississippi, 1930-1965; died, Ocean Springs.

## *Fall Pin Oaks with Birds*

c. 1945
Watercolor on paper, 25 x 19 inches
1990.0001

The watercolor at hand, a rare example of a large-scale work by Anderson, is one of several he created in his so-called "Oldfields" period. By the time he created it, he had already suffered his first serious siege of schizophrenia, had been hospitalized, and had begun a pattern of painting, writing, and visiting Horn Island off the Gulf Coast near Ocean Springs, Mississippi, that characterized his career. It was this exercise, Redding Sugg has suggested, that accounts for the "superb fulfillment and productivity which he chronicled in the logs and achieved in the drawings and paintings" (p. xv).

Neither critic nor historian, nor the informed viewer, can ever truly separate what may be known about an artist's life and an artist's work. In the case of Walter Anderson, where a strongly disassociational theme recurs in his images, the task of visual assessment is made all the more difficult. The extent to which his art acted as a kind of therapy, if not an actual cure, is most apparent in his naturalistic works. These, while densely patterned and obsessively detailed, are very beautiful celebrations drawn "in ecstasy," as he once remarked in his journal. *Fall Pin Oaks with Birds* is rendered with the strong recursive line and primary color typical of Anderson's Oldfields period. Though a symbolic observation of nature, it is representational in the most literal sense, devoid of atmosphere, and, ultimately, of any real sense of place. As a compelling study in line, it can hardly be surpassed, and therein rests Anderson's genius.

In many respects, the art of Walter Anderson is as deceptively simple, and therefore as elusive, as the art of Vincent van Gogh. Both were more than slightly disconnected from this world. While this may be a suitable role for the artist, the burden of mental illness lends their works a passionate intensity that transcends the pretty flowers, ripe fields, and gentle wildlife they loved to paint. The art of Walter Anderson is not a mirror of nature. It is a reflection of what he saw in the mirror, and what he was able to render, with superb craft and highly appealing visual awareness.

### PROVENANCE
From the estate of the artist; to Luise Ross Gallery, New York; by purchase to Southeastern Newspapers Corporation; by gift to Morris Museum of Art.

### LITERATURE
Anderson, Agnes Grinstead. *Approaching the Magic Hour: Memories of Walter Anderson.* Jackson, Mississippi, 1989.

Anderson, Walter Inglis. *The Horn Island Logs of Walter Anderson.* Edited and with an introduction by Redding Sugg, Jr. Memphis, Tennessee, 1973.

Brooks Memorial Art Gallery. *The World of Walter Anderson, 1903-1905.* Memphis, Tennessee.

Burton, Marda Kaiser. "Portraitist of Nature." *Horizon* (March 1982).

Donaldson, Susan. "Forsaking the Certainty of Shore: Walter Anderson and the Loneliness of Horn Island." *The Southern Quarterly* 24, nos. 1 and 2 (Fall-Winter 1985).

Pennington, Estill Curtis. "Walter Anderson in New Orleans." *The Arts Quarterly,* New Orleans Museum of Art (Summer 1988).

Pichard, Mary Anderson Stebly. *Sea-Earth-Sky: The Art of Walter Anderson.* Jackson, Mississippi, 1980.

Sugg, Redding, Jr. *Walter Anderson's Illustrations of Epic and Voyage.* Carbondale, Illinois, 1980.

———. *A Painter's Psalm: The Mural in Walter Anderson's Cottage.* Memphis, Tennessee, 1978.

Thompson, Carole E. *An American Master: Walter Anderson of Mississippi.* Memphis Brooks Museum of Art, Memphis, Tennessee, 1988.

Virginia Museum. *Painting in the South: 1564-1980.* Richmond, 1983.

### ARCHIVAL SOURCES
Anderson family archives, Shearwater Pottery Compound, Ocean Springs, Mississippi.

Mississippi Department of History and Archives, Jackson.

Walter Anderson Museum of Art, Research and Study Center, Ocean Springs, Mississippi.

### EXHIBITION HISTORY
"Walter Anderson: Watercolors and Drawings," Luise Ross Gallery, New York City, September 25-November 1, 1986; "The Watercolorists: Walter Anderson and His Peers," Vanderwoude Tananbaum Gallery, New York City, September 14-October 29, 1988.

Twentieth-Century Art

Following the First World War, certain intellectual strains that had been fermenting in the Southern mind for two generations surged to the fore in an explosive cultural boom. To this point, most cultural historians have regarded the Southern renascence as a strictly literary phenomenon. While it is true that the great Southern writers account for the remarkable substance of this movement, their activities correspond in time with the rise of truly remarkable indigenous Southern painters.

Keep in mind that this cultural awakening took place in the midst of the international modernist movement and at a moment in history when critics like H.L. Mencken could refer to the South as a "Sahara" of the Beaux Arts. This Southern renascence, so called by the Nashville Agrarians, was neither derivative nor interpretive of international modernism; rather it was a truly original expression of the Southern character.

Though the visual evidence should be explored in far greater depth, it is tempting to posit that abstraction, as a painterly form, never really took root in the South. Southern painters, like Southern writers, seem to have been enchanted by the narrative possibilities of the local scene. What we see in so much modern Southern painting is a complex tapestry of naturalistic and grotesque impulses that seize the imagination with a hungry eye, devouring the entire setting before it, and spinning back those fantastic tales Southerners love to tell.

## MARIE HULL

1890-1980

### Blue Parrots, Florida

c. 1927, signed lower right
Oil on canvas, 25⅛ x 25⅛ inches
1989.01.082

**PROVENANCE**
From the artist to Roy Wilkinson, Jackson, Mississippi;
to Knoke Galleries, Atlanta; by purchase to Robert
Powell Coggins Collection; by purchase to
Southeastern Newspapers Corporation; by gift to
Morris Museum of Art.

**LITERATURE**
Norwood, Malcolm M., Elias Virginia McGehee, and
William S. Hayne. *The Art of Marie Hull.* Jackson,
Mississippi, 1975.
    . *Marie Hull 1890-1980 Her Inquiring Vision.*
Cleveland, Mississippi, 1990.
Virginia Museum. *Painting in the South: 1564-1980.*
Richmond, 1983.

**ARCHIVAL SOURCES**
Delta State University Libraries, Cleveland,
Mississippi.
Eudora Welty Public Library, Jackson, Mississippi.
Lauren Rogers Museum of Art, Laurel, Mississippi.

Born, Summit, Mississippi; studied, Pennsylvania Academy of Fine Arts with Hugh Breckinridge, 1912, and at the Art Students League, New York City, with Frank Vincent Dumond, 1922; active in the Jackson, Mississippi, area, 1914-1980; died, Jackson.

During the 1920s, Marie Hull lived in Florida, where, according to Malcolm Norwood, she delighted in painting exotic birds. The time in Florida followed her period of study in New York at the Art Students League where, like Catherine Wiley and Helen Turner, she studied with Frank Vincent Dumond. Hull's parrots have a wildly Fauve feel and color – vibrant, close to the picture plane and highly decorative. In the course of her long life, Hull became the best-known figure in the small, but deeply committed, art world of rural Mississippi. As an artist, teacher and leader of that community, she encouraged widespread support for the arts in a state whose complex history often disguises its wealth of artists and writers.

Hull's personal philosophy was charmingly forthright: "I am fortunate to have discovered a long time ago what I wanted to do and to have continued in doing it in spite of obstacles or the attraction of other activities. The real reward in art is not the opinion of others. It is the ability to express oneself in one's own way. Of course, I had to earn that right by study, study, and more study and giving up many superficial activities to paint instead. Through the years my interest in painting and drawing and my endeavor to discover what constituted quality in art and attempt to achieve those things has been a never-ending activity. Through it all, I have clearly seen that creativity and quality are the essential things in art," (*Inquiring Vision*, p. 7).

## WADE WHITE

b. 1909

Born, Waterbury, Connecticut; studied at Yale University and at the Art Students League, New York; active in Charleston, South Carolina, during the 1930s.

### *Ravenel & Rivers Street, Charleston, South Carolina*

1934, signed and dated lower left
Oil on canvas, 29½ x 38 inches
1990.091

Wade White had been absent from the national art scene for more than fifty years when gallery owner Janet Marqusee "rediscovered" him at the age of 80. Marqusee immediately recognized the quality of formal training and intuitive associations of the artist, for whom she held a one-man show in New York in 1990. At that time she offered a superb assessment of his talent to the Fairfield, Connecticut, *Citizen-News*, noting especially his relationship to the Precisionist movement of Sheeler, Demuth and O'Keefe:

"Classically ordered, and conceived in a sensibility that pared down all excess, their work succeeded in altering our general perception of the American environment. The line is flawless, and little brushwork is in evidence. Simplification of form and carefully reasoned abstract organization are among the stylistic hallmarks most evident in this group of painters. Wade White's works reflect a definite and distinct connection with this movement. Typically, his very personal sense of form and color combines Precisionist subject matter – the buildings of rural and industrial America and the objects and surroundings of daily life – with a simplified, angularized formalism, thus placing him squarely within this grand tradition of Formalism which eliminated ornament and evolved an imagery notable for its essential coolness."

While White was not a Southern artist, he is a good example of an artist who brings a specific style and sensibility to a Southern setting. While Marqusee finds White's paintings to be "cool" in their color tonalities, they are, by comparison to the evanescent works of the Charleston Renaissance, rather bright and hot. *Ravenel & Rivers* is a rare example of a precisionist view of a scene of Southern urban realism. While devoid of the literary implications of much twentieth-century Southern art, it does quite brilliantly capture a specific sense of place.

#### PROVENANCE
From the artist to the Janet Marqusee Gallery, New York; to Artists' Chambers Gallery, Hamden, Connecticut; by purchase to Southeastern Newspapers Corporation; by gift to Morris Museum of Art.

#### LITERATURE
Marqusee, Janet. *Wade White: 1930s Precisionist.* New York, 1990.

Wagner, Addie. "Fairfield 'Precisionist' rediscovered at age 80." Fairfield (Connecticut) *Citizen-News,* January 17, 1990.

#### ARCHIVAL SOURCES
Mattatuck Historical Society, Waterbury, Connecticut.

#### EXHIBITION HISTORY
"Wade White: 1930s Precisionist." Janet Marqusee Gallery, January 1990.

## ANNE TAYLOR NASH

1884-1968

*Two Women*

c. 1935
Oil on canvas, 40 x 40 inches
1990.120

Born, Pittsboro, North Carolina; studied at the Gibbes Gallery, Charleston, South Carolina; with Elizabeth O'Neill Verner, 1924, and in various short courses at the Pennsylvania Academy and the New England School of Fine Arts; active in Charleston, and in Savannah, Georgia, 1931-1937, and 1948-1968; died, Savannah.

Anne Taylor Nash's boldly developed figurative paintings, created during her period of intensive productivity, 1931 to 1937, are penetrating expressions of a mainstream American format. In the manner of such American masters as Leon Kroll and Kenneth Hayes Miller, she deploys a compositional format that balances the complexity of figural placement, in this instance, leaning back as well as into the picture plane, with a very serious, sophisticated palette. While modernist in intent, this work also has that alluring quality of the baroque period, drawing the viewer into the setting, while obscuring narrative implication. It is a well-developed work from an artist of great promise whose full potential may never have been realized because of family obligations.

**PROVENANCE**
From the estate of the artist to John Petty, Columbia, South Carolina; by purchase to Robert Powell Coggins Collection; to the Robert Powell Coggins Art Trust; by purchase to Morris Museum of Art.

**LITERATURE**
Chambers, Bruce. *Art and Artists of the South.* Columbia, South Carolina, 1984.

**ARCHIVAL SOURCES**
Center for the Study of Southern Painting, Morris Museum of Art.

Telfair Academy of Arts and Sciences, artist's files, Savannah, Georgia.

## PAMELA HART VINTON BROWN RAVENEL

1888-?

### Southern Gothic

c. 1935, signed lower right
Oil on canvas, 30 x 40 inches
1989.01.158

Born, Brookline, Massachusetts; studied at the Maryland Institute in Baltimore with Edwin Whiteman; active in the South at St. Mary's, Georgia, during the 1930s; died ?

While little is known about either the life or career of Pamela Ravenel, certain deductions about this painting can be made from the visual evidence at hand. Precisely who named it *Southern Gothic* is intriguing, for that title is somewhat misleading. The Southern Gothic literary motif is concerned with decay and a flagrant failure to accept the realities of the present, dwelling instead in the faded glories of the antebellum past. What we have here is not "gothic" at all. The painting actually reads like a compendium of personalities, which may, indeed, recall "certain literary motifs of William Faulkner and Erskine Caldwell" as Chambers suggests (p.108). Both Faulkner and Caldwell were concerned with capturing the flavor of a picaresque type. So we see here. On the far left, a virile young man stares out from the picture plane with sullen self-confidence tinged with only the slightest suggestion of unease. Next, a wise and amiable older man benignly confronts the viewer with the air of a well-versed raconteur. The third man has a thinly masked critical look, staring straight on, suspicious of outsiders. Finally, a female figure. Doesn't it make perfect sense that her forthright gaze and wistful engagement reveal a clear self-portrait of the artist?

**PROVENANCE**
From the artist to a private collection in St. Mary's, Georgia; to Terry Lowenthal, Savannah, Georgia; by purchase to Robert Powell Coggins Collection; by purchase to Southeastern Newspapers Corporation; by gift to Morris Museum of Art.

**LITERATURE**
Chambers, Bruce. *Art and Artists of the South.* Columbia, South Carolina, 1984.

**EXHIBITION HISTORY**
"Art and Artists of the South: The Robert Powell Coggins Collection," 1984-1986. (See note on catalog organization for complete exhibition schedule.)

## CHARLES SHANNON

b. 1914

Born, Montgomery, Alabama; studied at Emory University and the Cleveland School of Art; active in the Montgomery, Alabama, area since 1937.

### Saturday Evening

1937
Oil on canvas, 34 x 24 inches
1989.01.175

Shannon's interest in the black community is best known through his discovery of and friendship with the self-taught artist Bill Traylor. But his interest in black subject matter for his own painting began in the summer of 1935. While Shannon was attending the Cleveland School of Art, he received a lucrative portrait commission. "With that and my uncle's donation of a piece of land on his plantation – a dream borne out by Cleveland's winters was realized – a log cabin studio in the backwoods of Alabama. My plans to settle there and paint did not materialize; but it was the experiences of that summer sharpened by the perspective gained in the North that I began to feel what this country down here really meant to me. I worked with the Negroes in building my cabin for two months – cutting down trees; snaking them with mules to the site of the cabin – building it. I went to their churches with them, to their dances and drank with them – I saw expressions of primitive souls. I came to love this land – the plants and people that grew from it. My last year in Cleveland, filled with this newly realized beauty – I stayed out of school most of the year and painted Negroes and the deep South from my imagination." (Seligmann catalog, quoting a letter of Charles Shannon dated April 10, 1938.)

*Saturday Evening* dates from this period. It is not a figure study so much as a swaying, rhythmic tribute to the spontaneous interaction of the subjects themselves.

**PROVENANCE**
From the artist by purchase to Robert Powell Coggins Collection; by purchase to Southeastern Newspapers Corporation; by gift to Morris Museum of Art.

**LITERATURE**
Chambers, Bruce. *Art and Artists of the South.* Columbia, South Carolina, 1984.

Gingold, Diana. *Charles Shannon: Paintings and Drawings.* Montgomery, Alabama, 1971.

Jacques Seligmann and Company. *Charles Shannon, Paintings of the South.* New York City, 1938.

Maresca, Frank and Roger Ricco. *Bill Traylor, His Art - His Life.* New York City, 1991.

Virginia Museum. *Painting in the South: 1564-1980.* Richmond, 1983.

**ARCHIVAL SOURCES**
Smithsonian Institution Fine Arts Library, artist's files.

**EXHIBITION HISTORY**
"Art and Artists of the South: The Robert Powell Coggins Collection," 1983-1984. (See note on catalog organization for complete schedule.)

## WILL HENRY STEVENS

1881-1949

*Still Life: Flowers with Distant Mountain*

c. 1940
Oil on canvas, 36½ x 30½ inches
1990.121

Born, Vevay, Indiana; studied at the Cincinnati Art Academy, 1901-1904; active in New Orleans and in Asheville, North Carolina, 1920-1949; died, New Orleans.

After 1922, Stevens began to spend regular, prolonged periods of time at his mountain retreat in Asheville, North Carolina. Many of the works that Stevens created there and on his sketching trips to Tennessee clearly indicate his subtle transformation into a non-objective artist. Others, such as this large still life, give evidence of Stevens' firm grounding in representationalism. While the naturalistic elements in this work are readily identifiable, contemplation of the subtle color variations, balanced by the lunging depth of the frontal composition, results in a more challenging visual interaction than may have been initially imagined.

It was the potential for this response that intrigued a reviewer for the *Cincinnati Times Star* on Christmas Day, 1938, who found in the artist's work "beautiful harmonies and subtle gradations of tone, exquisite designs, sometimes abstract and sometimes made up of living objects and a keen sense of good taste . . . . There is an underlying mood in everything that he does, and through his talent he makes us feel the emotion which he is feeling, regardless of subject matter."

**PROVENANCE**
From the estate of the artist to New Morning Gallery, Asheville, North Carolina; by purchase to Robert Powell Coggins Collection; to Robert Powell Coggins Art Trust; by purchase to Morris Museum of Art.

**LITERATURE**
Kelly, James C. *The South on Paper.* Spartanburg, South Carolina, 1985.

Lehman, Bernard. *Will Henry's Nature: The Pictorial Ideas of W.H. Stevens.* Unpublished manuscript, 1947-48. Tulane University Archives, New Orleans.

North, Percy. "Nature's Spirit in the Abstractions of Will Henry Stevens." *SECAC Review* (1989).

. *Visions of an Inner Life, Abstractions by Will Henry Stevens.* Emory University Museum of Art and Archaeology, Atlanta, 1988.

Pennington, Estill Curtis. *Downriver: Currents of Style in Louisiana Painting 1800-1950.* Gretna, Louisiana, 1991.

Poesch, Jessie. *Will Henry Stevens.* Greenville County Museum of Art, Greenville, South Carolina, 1987. (Contains the definitive bibliography to date.)

. "Will Henry Stevens…Modern Mystic: Beginnings to 1921." *The Southern Quarterly* 25, no. 1 (Fall 1986).

Virginia Museum. *Painting in the South: 1564-1980.* Richmond, 1983.

York, Richard T. *Will Henry Stevens (1881-1949): A Modernist's Response to Nature.* Richard York Gallery, New York, 1987.

**ARCHIVAL SOURCES**
Historic New Orleans Collection, curatorial files.

Howard-Tilton Memorial Library, Special Collections and Louisiana Collection, Tulane University, New Orleans.

Indianapolis Museum of Art archives.

McDowell Collection, Stevens family archives, Asheville, North Carolina.

New Orleans Museum of Art, curatorial files.

## FRANK LONDON

1876-1945

Born, Pittsboro, North Carolina; studied at the University of North Carolina, the Pratt Institute and the William Merritt Chase School of Art, New York City; active in Woodstock, New York, with frequent visits to North Carolina throughout his career. Died, New York City.

### *Tyranny of Survival*

1943, signed and dated lower left
Oil on canvas, 42 x 30 inches
1992.010

**PROVENANCE**
From the estate of the artist to his son, Marsden London; to Allison Gallery, New York City; by purchase to Morris Museum of Art.

**LITERATURE**
Tomlin, Bradley Walker. *Frank London, A Retrospective Showing of His Paintings.* Woodstock, New York, 1948.

Williams, Ben F. "Frank London: Retained in Symbol," in *Vital Objects, A Traveling Exhibition of Paintings and Drawings of Frank London.* Tarboro, North Carolina, 1989.

**ARCHIVAL SOURCES**
Center for the Study of Southern Painting, Morris Museum of Art.

Marsden London papers, Darien, Connecticut.

**EXHIBITION HISTORY**
"Frank London, A Retrospective Showing of His Paintings," Woodstock, New York, 1948, Mint Museum of Art, Charlotte, North Carolina, 1949; "Vital Objects: A Traveling Exhibition of Paintings and Drawings of Frank London," Hobson Pittman Memorial Gallery, Tarboro, North Carolina, July 15-August 27, 1989 and subsequently on tour throughout North Carolina until September 30, 1989. See publication for complete itinerary.

London spent most of his early career as an artist and illustrator in rather traditional American modes. However, in his maturity, he began to create a series of works in which time and space mingle with thematic concerns of "memory and desire" to quote T.S. Eliot. These late works are most impressive, especially when related to certain Southern literary developments in the same period.

When his works toured in the South after his death, these connections were not wasted on his more perceptive Southern contemporaries. In a truly remarkable letter, written on Thanksgiving Day 1948 and now in the Morris Museum of Art archives, Lucile Blanch, an art historian and curator at Wesleyan College in Macon, Georgia, shared her thoughts about London with his son:

"The show is an excellent lesson in making the student aware of the American tradition in art; it helps make him feel his connections, way back in the beginning of painting and living in our country. The American flavor is more truly carried on in our art through a sensitivity to its essence rather than in the more self conscious attitude of Wood, Benton and of Curry. I pointed out a fraternity in your father's painting with the literature of Faulkner, Poe, Lanier and even Tom Wolfe – notice these are all Southern writers, and not of the same time. Naturally we pondered long over the symbolism and its connection with a philosophy of life, and also with character traits, such as wit, irony, etc.

"There are a few things that seem to me inherent in all the work which point out a basic view of life in this world. Your father's use of the large solid base structure conveys a sense of indestructibility and therefore leads to thoughts of timelessness and eternity. Over it drifts the lush, the fragile, the soft, the short-lived, the small, the fanciful – in other words, our short span of life in relation to eternity. We are lush, and spread over this old globe covering its timelessness with our contemporary energy and activity and hasten to our decay – a fertile rot for the seeds of new life. We are the moss, the flowers, the flexible trivia playing over the solid masonry of the paintings."

## PAUL NINAS

1903-1964

Born, Cape Girardeau, Missouri; studied, University of Nebraska, Robert College of Constantinople, the Royal Academy of Vienna, the Beaux Arts Academy of Paris, France and in the atelier of Andre L'Hote, Paris, c. 1920-1924; active in New Orleans, 1932-1968; died, New Orleans.

### *Abstraction*

c. 1940
Oil on canvas, 47½ x 61 inches
1989.05.262

As a young man, Ninas explored the front-line art world of Paris in the '20s before taking up residence in New Orleans on a whim in 1932. Once settled there, however, he became an important fixture of the local art community, both as a teacher at the seminal Arts and Crafts Club and as a new-wave abstract painter. Unlike his contemporary Will Henry Stevens, Ninas lunged into the modern movement with unabashed vigor. One local critic, Margaret Dixon of the *Morning Advocate*, spoke with the voice of the people when she reviewed an exhibition of his abstractions in the late '30s. Most viewers, she felt, "would look askance at the abstractions, which will represent nothing at all to most of the visitors."

The Delgado Museum of Art in New Orleans sponsored a showing of important works by Picasso in December 1940, which seems to have made a lasting impression upon Ninas. Thereafter, his work becomes increasingly abstract. Many have the feel of analytic cubist landscapes and still lifes, breaking up the surface space into a series of decorative cubes or triangles filled with highly stylized birds and color variations. Kathleen Orillion has written that works like the abstract at hand "float in an ambiguous space of delicate and subtle harmonies of color and light. These seemingly childlike naive works may have resulted from years of teaching painting and drawing to children. He often remarked that he encouraged children's intuitive sense of design and color and admired their freshness and spontaneity" (p. 8).

Yet Ninas never saw himself as a radical abstract expressionist. "What baffles me is WHY everyone jumps into the mainstream of Abstract E. or Action painting. With the immense volume of mediocre, poor, fair art being produced, even the few good painters can create only a small ripple and I, for one, look askance at most of these. What a lot of big canvases the next generation will inherit to cut up and paint over" (Orillion, p. 9).

### PROVENANCE

From the estate of the artist to Downtown Gallery, New Orleans; by purchase to Southeastern Newspapers Corporation; by gift to Morris Museum of Art.

### LITERATURE:

Early, Eleanor. "Gave Up The Most Beautiful Model in Paris for Art on a Tropic Isle." *Every Week* magazine (1930).

Heintzen, Harry. "Meet the Pilot of Flight to Fancy." *The Times-Picayune/New Orleans States Item* magazine, October 19, 1947.

Orillion, Kathleen. *Paul Ninas 1903-1964.* Louisiana Arts and Science Center, Baton Rouge, 1986.

Pennington, Estill Curtis. *Downriver: Currents of Style in Louisiana Painting 1800-1950.* Gretna, Louisiana, 1991.

### ARCHIVAL SOURCES

Downtown Gallery, New Orleans.

Historic New Orleans Collection.

Howard-Tilton Memorial Library, Louisiana Collection, Tulane University, New Orleans.

## LAMAR DODD

b. 1909

Born, Fairburn, Georgia; studied, Georgia Institute of Technology, and with Boardman Robinson at the Art Students League, New York, 1928; active in Birmingham, Alabama, c. 1930-1937, and in Athens, Georgia since 1937.

### *Bargain Basement*

1937, signed lower right
Oil on canvas, 46 x 55 inches
1992.033

**PROVENANCE**
From the artist to the University of Georgia Foundation; by purchase to David S. Ramus Ltd., Atlanta; by purchase to Morris Museum of Art.

**LITERATURE**
Collier, Graham, "Lamar Dodd: Serene and Clear." *American Artist* 44 (June 1980).

David S.Ramus Ltd. *Lamar Dodd: Monhegan Watercolors.* Atlanta, Georgia, 1988.

Dodd, Lamar. "A Juryman Speaks." *College Art Journal* 1 (Spring 1951).

High Museum of Art. *Lamar Dodd: A Retrospective Exhibition.* Athens, Georgia, 1970.

Thomas, Howard. "Lamar Dodd: Southern Painter." *American Artist* 10 (February 1946).

Virginia Museum. *Painting in the South: 1564-1980.* Richmond, 1983.

Wheeler, Monroe. *Painters and Sculptors of Modern America.* New York City, 1942.

**EXHIBITION HISTORY**
"Lamar Dodd: Home," Georgia Museum of Art, Athens, March 8-25, 1990.

Always experimental and sensitively attuned to important trends in the avant-garde, Lamar Dodd has created a body of work spanning more than fifty years of teaching and painting in Georgia. Like other artists of the American scene during the decade of the 1930s, he was concerned with figurative painting carefully composed to give a full sense of place, in the manner of Thomas Hart Benton.

Benton and his fellow Regionalists John Stuart Curry and Grant Wood, "aimed at capturing the image of America's heartland, and (had) a nostalgic interest in preserving disappearing local types," in the words of Barbara Rose in her seminal work, *American Art Since* 1900. While Rose is undoubtedly correct in her assertion of the Regionalist political agenda, her point of view may be further expanded by consideration of the same movement in the South. Regionalism also responded to the climate of change brought about by the Great Depression,which was even more severe in the South. Regionalist artists, seeking to affirm so-called "traditional values," created scene paintings imbued with enormous vitality.

*Bargain Basement* seethes with that sense of vitality, enhanced by a curious mannerist composition, as seen in the vivid proximity of the bold female figure turning toward the picture plane. Her rather elegant air of well-dressed serenity is juxtaposed with the frantic activity of the shoppers spread out across the middle and background of the work. Dodd is said to have painted this work of an Alabama department store toward the end of his stay in that state. It reflects his assimilation of the figurative tradition of the Art Students League in New York, especially the teaching of Benton, and the lingering influence of Kenneth Hayes Miller. In many respects, it is his best painting: ambitious, lively, and quite well-developed.

# MARION SIMS SOUCHON

1871-1954

Born, New Orleans; academically trained as a medical doctor and largely self-taught as an artist, but with exposure to the Arts and Crafts Club of New Orleans; active as a painter in New Orleans from the early 1930s until his death; died, New Orleans.

## Maison Maurice

c. 1945
Oil on board, 28 x 22 inches
1990.111

Souchon was a gifted amateur artist whose actual profession was that of a surgeon. In 1941 he came to the attention of *Time* magazine, whose art critic found his work to be "Van Gogh-like pictures of hot, shadowless Louisiana cornfields, quaint, warm-colored, old-worldly interiors, and fanciful, childlike coloristic riots…." Hyphens aside, there is a ring of contemporary truth in the assessment, although it seems more likely that Souchon's sources were the Fauves' rebellious colors and Bonnard's placid domestic scenes.

*Maison Maurice* is a flat-figure study set in a shallow space enlivened, indeed, by "coloristic riot." Apparently, Souchon found anatomical composition trying. Again from *Time:* "because he finds meticulous draughtsmanship a bore, he doesn't even bother to finish the faces in his figures but leaves them eyelessly blank. But the people in Surgeon Souchon's paintings need faces no more than a poem needs footnotes. Effusive and bubbling as Oldster Souchon himself, they make their point not by depicting anything in particular, but by the sheer joyousness of their color."

Charmingly disarming as this peer found Souchon to be, to current eyes the vacant figures are slightly more disturbing. Pittman's faceless figures are dramatic reminders of the presence of the past in the present. Souchon's paintings have taken on a more didactic edge with the passing of time, an echo of the vapid formal atmosphere of the hierarchic New Orleans from which they come. In Pittman, figural form follows the function of intellectual disassociation, tinged with regret and remembrance. In Souchon, form is a nameless hostage, a poorly paid walk-on player in a drama where function has been abandoned to form.

**PROVENANCE**
From the estate of the artist to the Tilden-Foley Gallery, New Orleans; by purchase to Southeastern Newspapers Corporation; by gift to Morris Museum of Art.

**LITERATURE**
"Painting Doctor." *Time* magazine, December 29, 1941.

Pennington, Estill Curtis. *Downriver: Currents of Style in Louisiana Art 1800-1950.* Gretna, Louisiana, 1991.

**ARCHIVAL SOURCES**
Historic New Orleans Collection, curatorial files.

Works Progress Administration Papers, New Orleans Museum of Art.

## ROBERT GWATHMEY

1903-1988

Born, Richmond, Virginia; studied at the Pennsylvania Academy of Fine Arts; made annual summer trips to Virginia for subject matter throughout his career; died, Amagansett, Long Island, New York.

### *Reflections*

c. 1950, signed upper right
Oil on canvas, 26¾ x 32 inches
1992.024

**PROVENANCE**
Christie's Auction No. 7414, Lot 248; by purchase to Morris Museum of Art.

**LITERATURE**
Ingersoll, Jonathan. *Robert Gwathmey.* St. Mary's City, Maryland, 1976.

Piehl, Charles K. "Anonymous Heroines: Black Women as Heroic Types in Robert Gwathmey's Art." *Heroines of Popular Culture.* Bowling Green, Ohio, 1987.

. "Robert Gwathmey: The Social and Historical Context of a Southerner's Art in the Mid Twentieth Century." *Arts in Virginia* 29, no. 1 (1989).

. "A Southern Artist at Home in the North: Robert Gwathmey's Acceptance of His Identity." *The Southern Quarterly* (Fall 1987).

. "The Southern Social Art of Robert Gwathmey." Transactions of the Wisconsin Academy of Science, *Arts and Letters* 73 (1985).

McCausland, Elizabeth. "Robert Gwathmey," *Magazine of Art* (April 1946).

Robeson, Paul. *Robert Gwathmey.* New York City, 1946.

Virginia Museum. *Painting in the South: 1564-1980.* Richmond, 1983.

**ARCHIVAL SOURCES**
Archives of American Art, Smithsonian Institution, Oral History Collection.

Gwathmey is best known for his series of paintings of rural Southern blacks, paintings that affirm their basic humanity even as they become expressive vehicles for the artist's vision of their isolation from mainstream modern society. Gwathmey's style is a fascinating amalgam of analytic cubism and flat planes of color, a style that Charles Piehl notes "reminded some critics of cloisonne and others of medieval stained-glass windows."

Though this work is not from Gwathmey's more familiar subject matter, it is perhaps the most quintessentially Southern image on a twentieth-century theme in this collection. The elderly belle, in her gown and tiara, staring fiercely into the mirror, is the moral equivalent, in visual terms, of Oscar Wilde's Dorian Gray. Searching for either youth or beauty, she finds neither — only the returned gaze of a distant past. She is, therefore, that symbol of the Old South that fascinated Southern writers at mid-century.

Faulkner's Miss Rosa Coldfield, for example, couldn't stop remembering the past long enough to live in the present. Tennessee Williams' Amanda Wingfield and Blanche DuBois wrapped themselves in elaborate manners and colorful stories to deny the harsh realities of life in slums far from the plantation. What these characters suggest is the struggle faced by the South in the hundred years following the war, to reconcile the powerful dynamics of an expressive culture with strong mythic undercurrents, to the material poverty of a people apart from the general prosperity of American life.

Ultimately though, the old dame looking in the mirror is most like Peter Taylor's heroine in *Miss Leonora When Last Seen.* Taylor makes an elderly teacher of old-fashioned ways become the symbol of a Southern past encroaching upon the Southern present. Clinging to an ancient way of dress and the quaint affectations of bygone days, Miss Leonora evokes in her students that same longing to understand her character that defines all those who seek to know the Southland itself: "Looking back on those days, I know that all along she was watching me and others like me for some kind of sign from us — any sign — that would make us seem worthy of knowing what we wanted to know about her."

## NELL CHOATE JONES

1879-1981

Born, Hawkinsville, Georgia; studied, c. 1925, at the Adelphia Academy, Brooklyn, New York; intermittently active in the South, but especially in Georgia 1936-1956; died, Brooklyn.

### Georgia Red Clay

1946, signed lower right
Oil on canvas, 25 x 30 inches
1989.01.094

Though a native Southerner from a family long entrenched in the history and tradition of the South, Nell Choate was taken to Brooklyn as a child and remained there for the rest of her life. Still, the powerful substance of the Southern scene never left her. "I was born here, I am a Southerner and that's all there is to it," she said in a 1979 newspaper interview in her hometown of Hawkinsville, Georgia.

Chambers attributes the cogent sense of place in Jones' Georgia landscapes to a renewal of that sense of being Southern that she experienced on her return to her hometown in 1936 for the burial of her sister. This trip would provide the inspiration for many of her drawings and paintings of the next two decades. "While she emphasizes the picturesque qualities of Southern life, her simplified forms, rhythmic designs, and intense though often somber colors combine to produce a unique and almost Expressionist sense of latent energies" (p. 143).

**PROVENANCE**
From the estate of the artist to the Marbella Gallery, New York; by purchase to Robert Powell Coggins Collection; by purchase to Southeastern Newspapers Corporation; by gift to Morris Museum of Art.

**LITERATURE**
Chambers, Bruce. *Art and Artists of the South.* Columbia, South Carolina, 1984.

"Confederate's Daughter Returns Home for Visit." *Hawkinsville Dispatch & News,* January 3, 1979.

Kelly, James C. *The South on Paper.* Spartanburg, South Carolina, 1985.

Sauls, James M. *Works on Paper from the Robert P. Coggins Collection of American Art.* Marietta, Georgia, 1984.

**ARCHIVAL SOURCES**
Archives of American Art, Smithsonian Institution.

Center for the Study of Southern Painting, Morris Museum of Art.

**EXHIBITION HISTORY**
"Paintings by Nell Choate Jones," Marbella Gallery, New York City, May 22-June 2, 1979; "Land of our Own: 250 Years of Landscape and Gardening Tradition in Georgia," Atlanta Historical Society, March 1-August 31, 1983; "Art and Artists of the South: The Robert Powell Coggins Collection," 1984-1986. (See note on catalog organization for complete exhibition schedule.)

## JOHN McCRADY

1911-1968

Born Canton, Mississippi; studied, University of Mississippi, Pennsylvania Academy of Fine Arts, New Orleans Arts and Crafts Club, Art Students League, New York City; active in New Orleans, 1932-1968; died, New Orleans.

### I Can't Sleep

1948, signed lower right
Multi-stage on canvas, 36 x 48 inches
1989.05.260

**PROVENANCE**
From the estate of the artist to Downtown Gallery, New Orleans; by purchase to Southeastern Newspapers Corporation; by gift to Morris Museum of Art.

**LITERATURE**
Marshall, Keith. *John McCrady 1911-1968.* New Orleans Museum of Art, 1975.

McCrady, John, Caroline Durieux, and Ralph Wickiser. *Mardi Gras Day.* New Orleans, 1948.

Pennington, Estill Curtis. *Downriver: Currents of Style in Louisiana Art 1800-1950.* Gretna, Louisiana, 1991.

────. *Look Away: Reality and Sentiment in Southern Art.* Atlanta, 1989.

Summers, Marion. "Studies in Contrast: Chauvinism and Truth," *The Daily Worker,* May 29, 1946.

Virginia Museum. *Painting in the South 1564-1980.* Richmond, 1983.

**ARCHIVAL SOURCES**
Butler Art Institute, Youngstown, Ohio.

Historic New Orleans Collection.

McCrady Papers, Mrs. John McCrady, New Orleans.

**EXHIBITION HISTORY**
"John McCrady 1911-1968," New Orleans Museum of Art, September 26-November 2, 1975, Mississippi Art Association, Jackson, February 8-March 21, 1976, Montgomery Museum of Fine Arts, Alabama, April 18-May 30, 1976, Paine Art Center, Oshkosh, Wisconsin, June 27-August 8, 1976.

An expressive, deeply personal mythos pervades much of McCrady's work in the period prior to 1948. During these years, from his days as a student in Oxford up to his full maturity as a painter in New Orleans, McCrady brought a sensibility with strong literary associations to the narrative intent of his art. Often his works depict the folk ways of black people living in rural areas. But in many instances they also depict the raucous, bohemian existence of life in the Vieux Carré of New Orleans. *I Can't Sleep* began as a drawing in 1933. McCrady began to work on the painting in 1936, but did not complete it until 1948, after an injurious article had appeared in the communist *Daily Worker*. It was that article's stinging criticism of McCrady's implicit racism that ended his narrative/genre phase.

Early in 1936, McCrady wrote to his friend Clyde Singer regarding his intentions for the painting. "I am cutting the building in two, showing the life inside as well as out. It's an interesting old place with patios and balconies. I'm showing myself on the ground floor, sitting up in bed with my hands over my ears trying to shut out the noise coming from a big party on the second floor. One of those parties given by Med. students. On the top attic floor a woman walks a bawling brat while her husband snores. Outside, the moon, stars, chimneys, smoke, etc. Sounds like too much stuff for one picture but I think I have fixed it so I can handle it all."

## AUGUSTA OELSCHIG

b. 1917

Born, Savannah, Georgia; studied with Emma Cheves Wilkins, 1935-37, and with Lamar Dodd at the University of Georgia, 1937-1939; active in Savannah throughout her career.

### *Play Ball*

c. 1955, signed upper left
Oil on canvas, 17 x 26 inches
1989.01.146

Following Oelschig's period of study with Horace Kallen at the New School for Social Research in New York, 1950-51, Lamar Dodd referred to her as "a talented and imaginative young artist with the tools to produce the very personal and regional scenes of Social consequence." Dodd was more devastatingly correct than he may have imagined, for much of Oelschig's art in the subsequent fifteen years dealt with the serious social injustice of Southern race relations. Many of her paintings concern black subjects. Some depict horrific, violent lynching scenes. Others essay the black presence in the same genre terms one finds in the works of Charles Shannon. All are far braver than the spirit of the times would have tolerated.

*Play Ball* has something of the feel of Paul Cadmus' various urban scenes. A seemingly simple straightforward interaction between children from different backgrounds carries a mildly unsettling undertone of fierce competition and spirited personal expression, as seen in the demonstrative faces of the subjects themselves. A full exploration of Oelschig's body of work may reveal yet another unsung genius of Southern painting in the middle of this century.

**PROVENANCE**
From the artist to Terry Lowenthal; by purchase to Robert Powell Coggins Collection; by purchase to Southeastern Newspapers Corporation; by gift to Morris Museum of Art.

**ARCHIVAL SOURCES**
Center for the Study of Southern Painting, Morris Museum of Art.

# HOBSON PITTMAN

1900-1972

Born, Epworth, North Carolina; studied at the Rouse Art School in Tarboro, North Carolina, and at the Pennsylvania State College and the Carnegie Institute; active in North and South Carolina throughout his career; died, Philadelphia.

## Garden Party

Undated, signed upper right
Oil on masonite panel, 29½ x 45⅝ inches
1990.128

Pittman was a North Carolina native who seems to have carried the Southern literary sensibility with him throughout his career. Like Faulkner's character Quentin Compson, he gives the impression of an individual with a well-honed remembrance of things past, which lingers like a vanquished spirit in his art. It is this quality that has attracted the attention of several acute critics and historians. Evan Turner sees Pittman as an painter of "opportunities lost. Commitments bypassed. Such are the sad mysteries of Hobson Pittman's large pictures" (p. 3). For Turner, paintings like the *Garden Party* represent "the ambivalence of … wandering figures, which are almost always women, dressed in a style vaguely suggesting that of the first years of this century. They do not explain, they do not commit, they exist, and however small the images, their presence is dominant."

Patrick Stewart, in his superb essay for the *Painting in the South* catalog, does not dwell upon Pittman's disassociational mood, but rather his direct evocation of the fleeting quality of the Southern imagination. Stewart finds in his art "the strong feeling of remembrance …but it is not a specific, easily understandable feeling. Pittman's (paintings) are attempts to recapture an other-worldly Southern past that perhaps exists only in fiction" (p. 131).

**PROVENANCE**
From the artist to a private collection in Philadelphia; to Babcock Galleries, New York; by purchase to Southeastern Newspapers Corporation; by gift to Morris Museum of Art.

**LITERATURE**
Hull, William. *The World of Hobson Pittman.* University Pennsylvania State Museum of Art, University Park, 1972.

Turner, Evan. *Hobson Pittman.* New York, 1970.

Virginia Museum. *Painting in the South: 1564-1980.* Richmond, 1983.

Williams, Ben F. *Hobson Pittman, Retrospective Exhibition: His Work since 1920.* North Carolina Museum of Art, Raleigh 1963.

**ARCHIVAL SOURCES**
Smithsonian Institution Fine Arts Library, artist's files.

## HENRY FAULKNER

### 1924-1981

### *Still Life with Golden Slipper*

c. 1965
Oil on masonite, 16⅞ x 18⅞ inches
1990.064

Born, Fountain Run, Kentucky; active in New Orleans, 1944-45, and in Lexington, Kentucky, 1955-1981; died, Lexington.

Faulkner's life was as tragicomic as it was outrageous, a Southern Gothic mixture of Tennessee Williams and Truman Capote at their most deranged. Faulkner's life was punctuated with bouts of madness, for which he was institutionalized, and periods of abandon, during which times he pursued the androgynous mysteries of transvestism. All the while he strove to be a creative personality, as expressed in his writings and painting. While he was entirely self-taught, his achievement is in the realm of mainstream modernism of the highly symbolic sort, and not in the idiosyncratic expressions that characterize the works of other Southern artists discussed in the subsequent section of this catalog.

Clearly, Faulkner was deeply influenced by the art of Marc Chagall. Like Chagall he uses a highly charged palette rich in pastels and primary color values that give his works a rather electric mood. Many of his paintings also feature symbolic animals, especially cats, which function like the sky-jumping goats in Chagall's art. Here, Faulkner combines the formal demands of traditional still-life painting with his own signature coloration. Each object is rendered with great intensity and commanding presence of the type the artist embodied in his own eccentric life in Lexington, Kentucky. While he won only slight recognition in his own lifetime, his art is becoming one of the hottest topics in mid-twentieth-century art in the South.

**PROVENANCE**
From the Lexington Antique Mall, Lexington, Kentucky; by purchase to Southeastern Newspapers Corporation; by gift to Morris Museum of Art.

**LITERATURE**
House, Charles. *The Outrageous Life of Henry Faulkner: Portrait of an Appalachian Artist.* Knoxville, Tennessee, 1988. (The "Note on the Sources" at the end of the volume provides a detailed account of all Faulkner primary materials.)

**ARCHIVAL SOURCES**
University of Tennessee Archives. Papers of Charles House pertaining to the biography of Henry Faulkner. Knoxville, Tennessee. (In recounting his methodological approach to Faulkner, House notes that "most of the materials (gathered), either originals or copies, are on file at the University of Tennessee Archives.")

# The Self-Taught Southern Artist

Early in this century, colonial revival critics and collectors focused their passions upon the works of artists from outside the academic, urban, and urbane mainstream. Initially, these individuals were referred to as "folk" artists, a term with a condescending agenda suggesting an illustrative quaintness that is an abiding American infatuation.

Acclaim for those artists, and appreciation of their works, is open to interpretation at several levels. Western culture since the romantic period has had an insatiable yearning for a "natural man" who grew and developed outside the oppressive shaping forces of material capitalism. While this yearning can reflect a worthy regard for unique personalities, it is also subject to becoming at best, trite, and at worst, camp.

The phrase "self-taught" is perhaps the more honest, objective, descriptive term. Like "folk," "outsider" has a hidden agenda preoccupied with who is in and who is out. "Visionary" is equally objectionable for its exclusion of the trained artist who may value his spiritual insights as much as the untrained artist.

The tremendous boom in interest in this field during the past ten years represents nothing short of a revolution in Southern art. The Southern self-taught artist currently occupies a position on the national stage unrivaled in the history of the plastic arts in the South.

# RALPH BREWER

1901-1975

Born, Bryan County, Georgia; educated at the Presbyterian Institute, Blackshear, Georgia; began to paint c. 1930 in Alexandria, Louisiana, where he lived after 1920; died, Alexandria.

## *Blowing Trees*

c. 1934
Kerosene thinned oil medium on cardboard,
11¼ x 22 inches
1989.08.286

At some point in the early 1930s, Ralph Brewer encountered the Louisiana artist Alexander John Drysdale while on a business trip to New Orleans. Although Brewer was a newspaperman by profession, he was an enthusiastic self-taught painter who turned out hundreds of works on the backs of the cardboard inserts from laundered shirts. His art follows two patterns: still-life works reminiscent of the subliminally suggestive painting of Redon and landscapes in the manner of Drysdale.

Within the canon of Brewer's landscape art, several recurring compositional conventions can be detected. His most obvious device is the placement of a group of trees alongside a stream flowing in a curvilinear manner from the foreground to the rear of the picture plane. Often these trees are bent, as if blown in a storm, and painted over with kinetic white pigment, as though rain, or even snow, were falling upon them. These works were painted in a medium very similar to Drysdale's kerosene thinned oil paint. A disturbing immediacy pervades Brewer's landscapes. These trees have a lonely, anxious quality, compounded by besieging winds and an isolated sense of space in which no human beings are ever seen.

PROVENANCE
By purchase from the artist's son, Foster Brewer of Houston, Texas, to Southeastern Newspapers Corporation; by gift to Morris Museum of Art.

LITERATURE
Brewer, Ralph Wright. "Flivering Through Dixie in 1921." Unpublished manuscript. Center for the Study of Southern Painting, Morris Museum of Art.

. "My Introduction to a Pirogue." Unpublished manuscript, Center for the Study of Southern Painting, Morris Museum of Art.

. "Put Your Money in the Ground." Unpublished manuscript, Center for the Study of Southern Painting, Morris Museum of Art.

Pennington, Estill Curtis. *Downriver: Currents of Style in Louisiana Painting 1800-1950*. Gretna, Louisiana, 1991.

ARCHIVAL SOURCES:
Miscellaneous clippings, manuscripts, slides of work, and an oral history conducted by Estill Curtis Pennington with the artist's son, Ralph Wright Brewer, Jr., are to be found in the Center for the Study of Southern Painting, Morris Museum of Art.

## MINNIE EVANS

1892-1987

Born, Long Creek, North Carolina; attended school through the sixth grade; active in the Wilmington, North Carolina, area throughout her career; died, Wilmington.

### *Ark of the Covenant*

c. 1966, signed lower right
Oil on canvasboard, 14½ x 19½ inches
1990.008

Evans' oft-quoted remark that God told her to "paint or die" is proof enough of the divine inspiration that pervades her work. A person of strong faith, Evans was a visionary of the highest order, an Old Testament type who saw her work as a symbolic expression of redemption. "I wanted God to create in me a clean heart and then renew the right spirit within me. That's what I prayed for and that's what He did" (McWillie, p. 62). Regina Perry has written that Evans' paintings are "essentially religious in inspiration and represent a world in which God, man, and nature are synonymous. God is sometimes represented as a winged figure with a wide multicolored collar and a rainbow halo. He is often surrounded by a proliferation of butterflies, eyes, trees, plants, and floral forms in a paradisiacal garden of brilliant colors."

**PROVENANCE**
From the artist to the Rev. and Mrs. William D. Eddy, North Carolina; to Luise Ross Gallery, New York; by purchase to Southeastern Newspapers Corporation; by gift to Morris Museum of Art.

**LITERATURE**
Hartigan, Lynda Roscoe. *Made with Passion*. Washington, D.C., 1990.

Khan, Mitchell D. *Heavenly Visions: The Art of Minnie Evans*. Raleigh, North Carolina, 1986.

Manley, Roger. *Signs and Wonders: Outsider Art Inside North Carolina*. Raleigh, North Carolina, 1989.

McWillie, Judith, et.al. *Another Face of the Diamond: Pathways Through the Black Atlantic South*. Atlanta, 1989.

Rosenak, Chuck and Jan. *Museum of American Folk Art Encyclopedia of Twentieth-Century American Folk Art and Artists*. New York City, 1990.

**EXHIBITION HISTORY**
"The Lost World of Minnie Evans," St. Clement's Church, New York City, May 1966; "Minnie Evans," Whitney Museum of American Art, New York City, July 3, 1975-August 3, 1975.

# CLEMENTINE HUNTER

1887-1988

Born, Hidden Hill Plantation, near Cloutierville, Louisiana; no formal schooling; began to paint c. 1940; active on Melrose Plantation throughout her career; died, near Melrose, Natchitoches, Louisiana.

## *Black Jesus*

1972, signed lower right
Oil on board, 23½ x 8⅞ inches
1990.024

In a somewhat mystical moment, Hunter once remarked to James Register, concerning the subject of this painting, "That's Black Jesus, and the angel ... I don't know if they black or white. 'Cause narly everybody says 'Black Jesus' so I thought I'd make him black like." Hunter was one of the first, and best known, of the self-taught black artists working in the rural South. Some have suggested that her art may have suffered from her fame. Late in her career she tended to reproduce, in mass quantity, her familiar scenes of rural blacks picking cotton. Religious imagery of this type is far more rare.

**PROVENANCE**
From the artist to Mrs. William Nolan, Natchitoches; to Mrs. Peter Tattersall; to the Tattersall-O'Brien Collection; to the Tattersall Gallery, Aiken, South Carolina; by purchase to Southeastern Newspapers Corporation; by gift to Morris Museum of Art.

**LITERATURE**
Mignon, Francois. *Plantation Memo: Plantation Life in Louisiana, 1950-70, and Other Matters.* Baton Rouge, Louisiana, 1972.

Vlach, John Michael. *The Afro-American Tradition in Decorative Arts.* Cleveland, Ohio, 1978.

Wilson, James. *Clementine Hunter, American Folk Artist.* Gretna, Louisiana, 1988. (Contains definitive bibliography to date.)

**ARCHIVAL SOURCES**
Black Women Oral History Project, Interview with Clementine Hunter, November 29, 1979, Schlesinger Library, Radcliffe College, Cambridge, Massachusetts.

James Register Collection, Francois Mignon Collection, Melrose Collection, Thomas N. Whitehead Collection. Cammie G. Henry Research Center, Eugene P. Watson Memorial Library, Northwestern State University of Louisiana, Natchitoches.

## MARGARET RAMSEY

b. 1932

### The Ice Cream Man

1982, signed lower left
Oil on canvas, 24 x 30 inches
1990.023

Born, Dublin, Georgia; attended Dublin schools and nursing school in Columbia, South Carolina, R.N. from Georgia Southwestern College, Americus; began painting in 1978; active in Augusta, Georgia.

Inspired by an outdoor art exhibit, Margaret Ramsey began making memory paintings at age 46. She uses her art to tell stories of her youth. She also provides a written narrative in a beautiful script:

"*The Ice Cream Man* materialized out of scenes I observed while sitting on the front porch of my house at 308 East Mary Street in Dublin, Georgia. One of my neighbors, Annie Mae Gillis, passed out on her job at the sewing factory and died at age 39. She was a member of a large family (mostly Country Folk) who came together on the day of her Funeral. It was a beautiful sunny Sunday afternoon and there were many adults and children on her porch, in front of her house, even spilling over into the street. The Children were playing on their skateboards, riding bicycles, wrestling, playing with their puppies and having fun.

"The grown ups were shaking hands, laughing, talking and hugging each other. The other neighbors were sitting on their porches watching the scenery and some of them, especially the Children, no doubt wanted to join the bereaved Family in their merriment. Then along came the Ice Cream Man in his delightfully decorated truck. There were pictures of colorful ice cream cones and Eskimo pies with popsicles adorning both sides and the back of his truck. Musical Chimes filled the air like those of an organ grinder. Many gathered around the Ice Cream man and his truck to make their tasty purchases. A beautiful loving sight to be seen."

PROVENANCE
Purchased from the artist by Southeastern Newspapers Corporation; by gift to Morris Museum of Art.

LITERATURE
Deriso, Christine. "Nurse's Artwork Makes Childhood Come Alive." *The Beeper.* Medical College of Georgia, August 25, 1987.

ARCHIVAL SOURCES
Center for the Study of Southern Painting, Morris Museum of Art.

## ZEBEDEE ARMSTRONG, JR.

b. 1911

Born, Thomson, Georgia; attended school through the eighth grade in McDuffie County schools; active in Thomson.

### *Box with Cups, Year of 1986*

1986
Polychrome found objects, 12½ x 10 inches
1991.011

From 1969 until 1982, Armstrong worked in the Thomson Box factory, an occupation that may account, in part, for the strong sense of encapsulation in his art. During this same period, in 1972 according to the Rosenaks, an angel appeared to him warning of the end of the world. From that time forth, his chronometric obsessions have led Armstrong to create hundreds of densely patterned boxes, containers, and calendars that express his sense of the imminent collapse of time as we have known it. It is tempting to compare Armstrong to the artist Joseph Cornell, who also experimented with the box form as a container for his fantasies on a theme of time. Both artists have a pronounced sense of moment, and both create an extensive, well-defined, metaphoric universe into which they project their own horological sensibility.

**PROVENANCE**
By purchase from the Red Piano Gallery, Hilton Head, South Carolina, to Southeastern Newspapers Corporation; by gift to Morris Museum of Art.

**LITERATURE**
Rosenak, Chuck and Jan. *Museum of American Folk Art Encyclopedia of Twentieth-Century American Folk Art and Artists.* New York City, 1990.

## RICHARD BURNSIDE

b. 1944

Born, Baltimore; attended Sterling High School, Greenville, South Carolina; active in Pendleton, South Carolina.

### *Pahro of Egipt*

c. 1985, signed lower right
Oil on corrugated board, 22¾ x 30½ inches
Robert Powell Coggins Art Trust,
Morris Museum of Art COG-0445

Images of kings and queens from a remote African past inhabit many of Burnside's paintings. His vibrant primary colors enhance the semiotic element of the work, animating the figures with a compelling presence. Spontaneous, and with no reference to anatomy or context, these faces float upon a surreal surface with the intensity of a glowing neon sign. The paint is very heavily applied and the faces often outlined in either a heavy impasto or with bits of pine cone applied to the surface. This outlining tends to emphasize the suggestion of royalty set apart, an iconographic implication whose deeper message remains unknown.

**PROVENANCE**
Purchased from the artist for the Robert Powell Coggins Collection; to Robert Powell Coggins Art Trust, Morris Museum of Art.

**LITERATURE**
Rosenak, Chuck and Jan. *Museum of American Folk Art Encyclopedia of Twentieth-Century American Folk Art and Artists.* New York City, 1990.

## MARY TILLMAN SMITH

b. 1904

Born, Brookhaven, Mississippi; minimal education in the Pleasantville Church School, Pleasantville, Mississippi; began to paint in 1980; active in Hazelhurst, Mississippi.

### *Red Figure on Blue*

c. 1978-88
House paint on corrugated tin
52¼ x 26⅞ inches
1990.134

Medium and support join in Smith's art to create a profound minimal expression. To this eye, her work is the clearest embodiment of certain recurring African semiotic motifs of the type many scholars suggest occur in self-taught art. Smith paints on corrugated tin, whose undulating surface creates a unique environmental statement. The rhythm of that surface is embellished with strong, warm color that is more subdued than the bright, hot primary shades favored by so many artists in this collection. Though it may be a forced observation, the effect recalls the African-influenced works of Picasso's earliest cubist period.

**PROVENANCE**
From the artist to American Primitive Gallery, New York City; by purchase to Southeastern Newspapers Corporation; by gift to Morris Museum of Art.

**LITERATURE**
McWillie, Judith, et. al. *Another Face of the Diamond: Pathways Through the Black Atlantic South.* New Visions Gallery, Atlanta, 1989.

Mhire, Herman, Andy Nacisse, and Maude Southwell Wahlman. *Baking in the Sun: Visionary Images from the South.* University of Southwestern Louisiana Art Museum, Lafayette, 1987.

Museum of York County. *Living Traditions: Southern Black Folk Art.* Rock Hill, South Carolina, 1991.

Rosenak, Chuck and Jan. *Museum of American Folk Art Encyclopedia of Twentieth-Century American Folk Art and Artists.* New York City, 1990.

## CHARLES KINNEY

b. 1906

Born, Vanceburg, Kentucky; minimal education in the Brewer School, Salt Lick, Kentucky; began to paint c. 1970; active in Vanceburg.

### We Saw 7 Rainbows 7 Suns This Day

1989, signed upper right
Watercolor and tempera on paper
22 x 28½ inches
1990.080

Kinney and his brother Noah, also an artist, began their retirement from farming and their careers by letting their old tobacco farm in northeastern Kentucky return to wilderness. This was all right with Charles, who always thought his log cabin homeplace was haunted anyway by a huge amorphous creature he often paints, called the "haint." This work is not about the haint, but about one of Kinney's other favorite subjects, memories of his youth. He recalls with great pleasure the day when summer showers passing with great speed through the countryside made possible the vision of repeated suns and rainbows through the mist of the afternoon.

**PROVENANCE**
From the artist to Art Jones Gallery, Cincinnati; by purchase to Morris Museum of Art.

**LITERATURE**
Rosenak, Chuck and Jan. *Museum of American Folk Art Encyclopedia of Twentieth-Century American Folk Art and Artists.* New York City, 1990.

## MOSE TOLLIVER

b. 1919

### *Black Crucifix with Birds*

Signed lower middle center
Enamel on plywood, 48 x 19¾ inches
1990.133

Born, Pike Road Community, Alabama; minimal education; began to paint in 1970; active in Montgomery, Alabama.

Tolliver is best known for his somewhat horrific, often densely erotic images rendered in a highly keyed palette. In many respects, his art is the most intense, and disconnected, self-taught art being created in the South today. The works tend to be finished with a strong black line around the edge, clearly demarcating the picture plane, and suspended from the pop-top tab of a beer can.

Regina Perry admires his sense of color: "Perhaps the most powerful aspect of Tolliver's paintings is his extraordinarily successful use of color. Although he paints exclusively with inexpensive house paint, his flat tones are never garish or discordant." As with Hunter, the crucifixion is an unusual topic for Tolliver. Painted with his typical interaction of three colors, it is enlivened by the floating, transcendental birds hovering about the lyrical form of the cross.

**PROVENANCE**
From the artist to American Primitive Gallery, New York City; by purchase to Southeastern Newspapers Corporation; by gift to Morris Museum of Art.

**LITERATURE**
Hartigan, Lynda Roscoe. *Made with Passion*. Washington, D.C., 1990.

Livingston, Jane and John Beardsley. *Black Folk Art in America 1930-1980*. Jackson, Mississippi, 1982. (Contains extensive bibliography.)

Mhire, Herman, Andy Nacisse, and Maude Southwell Wahlman. *Baking in the Sun: Visionary Images from the South*. University of Southwestern Louisiana Art Museum, Lafayette, 1987.

Museum of York County. *Living Traditions: Southern Black Folk Art*. Rock Hill, South Carolina, 1991.

Perry, Regina. *What It Is: Black American Folk Art from the Collection of Regina Perry*. Anderson Gallery, Virginia Commonwealth University, Richmond, 1982.

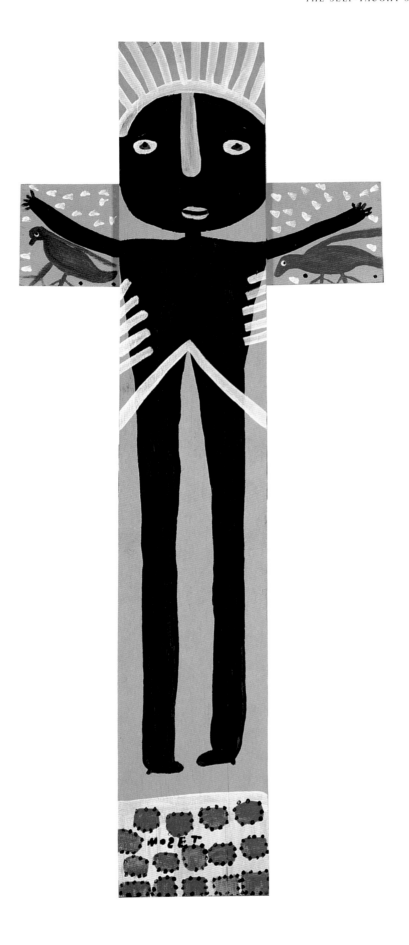

## LONNIE HOLLEY

b. 1950

Born, Birmingham, Alabama; attended school through the seventh grade, Princeton Elementary School, Birmingham; began to create art in 1979; active in Birmingham.

### *Eye Have the Hand that Holds the Staff for the Ancestor's Sake*

1989
Watercolor, tempera on paper, 22 x 28 inches
1990.026

Much of Holley's work celebrates the interconnected quality of time, by which the atavistic gifts of our ancestors inform each renewing cycle of subsequent generations. This renewal may be seen in his art. Holley has stated that "time, for me, works like a door. You have to go through time in order to be in it. It seems like one big cycle from within, like a spring. You start at the innermost part of the spring and you move outward as you grow. And, as you grow, this materialistic body, which is flesh, takes its place and acts; then it falls back to the beginning to re-create itself" (McWillie, p. 63). Renewal, in this work, may be symbolized by the recurrence of groups of three. The three eyes, three hands, and three sarcophagi arranged in a hieroglyphic configuration portend that renewal the artist seeks.

PROVENANCE
From the artist to American Primitive Gallery, New York City; by purchase to Southeastern Newspapers Corporation; by gift to Morris Museum of Art.

LITERATURE
McWillie, Judith, et. al. *Another Face of the Diamond: Pathways Through the Black Atlantic South*. New Visions Gallery, Atlanta, 1989.

Nosanow, Barbara Shissler. *More than Land or Sky: Art from Appalachia*. Washington, D.C., 1981.

Rosenak, Chuck and Jan. *Museum of American Folk Art Encyclopedia of Twentieth-Century American Folk Art and Artists*. New York City, 1990.

Southeastern Center for Contemporary Art. *Next Generation: Southern Black Aesthetic*. Winston-Salem, North Carolina, 1990.

# J. T. (JAKE) McCORD

b. 1945

*Winged Alligator*

1990, signed lower middle left
Acrylic on canvas, 16 x 20 inches
1991.007

Born, Thomson, Georgia; minimal education at Pleasant School, Thomson; began to paint in 1984; active in Thomson.

McCord left little doubt as to his inspiration when interviewed by Dale Hokrein: "I have three televisions on, and it looks like that helps me thinking it all up. It looks like that starts something that brightens my mind."

"Bright" certainly describes McCord's large, playful forms of fanciful animals and allegorical figures. Not all his subjects are demure, however. One recurring image is a rather racy lady clad in frilly underwear, who leers out from the picture plane with undisguised interest in the viewer. Often, these works are displayed in the front windows of the artist's home. "Whenever I paint a painting, I puts it up in the house. When I gets up the next morning, I looks up at what I done and it makes me feel good. Helps me make the day."

**PROVENANCE**
From the artist to Red Piano Gallery, Hilton Head, South Carolina; by purchase to Southeastern Newspapers Corporation; by gift to Morris Museum of Art.

**LITERATURE**
Hokrein, Dale. "Grass-cutting Artist Gains Notoriety." *The Augusta Chronicle,* June 3, 1991.

Rosenak, Chuck and Jan. *Museum of American Folk Art Encyclopedia of Twentieth-Century American Folk Art and Artists.* New York City, 1990.

# HOWARD FINSTER

b. 1916

Born, Valley Head, Alabama; attended school through the sixth grade at Violet Hill School, Valley Head; began to work as an artist in 1965; active in Summerville, Georgia.

## *Mona Lisa*

1987, signed and inscribed verso
Polychromed wood, 12½ x 7¼ x 4 inches
1990.078

Finster's art, motivated by a strong belief in the power of faith to redeem the individual soul, is an intense art of signs and symbols. His environmental composition, "Paradise Garden," outside his home in Summerville, Georgia, is considered one of the masterpieces of its type in the twentieth century. Finster often incorporates passages of didactic semiotics into his works. The Mona Lisa is a recurring image created by the artist within his conceptual realm of legendary figures. Inscribed upon this piece is the message:

"Mona Lisa By Howard Finster From God. Man Of Visions. Great People Are Remembered A Long Time-If You Get Your Name Recorded In Heaven You Will Be Remembered Forever You Will Never Be Forgotten Again Take The Very Words Of Jesus By Faith Study Them And You Can Become The Member Of God's Family Recorded In Heaven Sealed Forever And Ever This World Don't Have Enough Riches To Compare With God's Gift To You It Is Beyond Knowing Or Seeing What God Has For Those Who Keep His Sayings Don't Put Your Soul Off It Is Really All You Own Care For It."

**PROVENANCE**
From the artist to Art Jones Gallery, Cincinnati; by purchase to Southeastern Newspapers Corporation; by gift to Morris Museum of Art.

**LITERATURE**
Finster, Howard. *Man of Visions.* Atlanta, 1989.

, and Tom Patterson. *Howard Finster Stranger From Another World Man of Visions Now On This Earth.* New York City, 1989. (Contains extensive bibliography.)

Turner, J.E. *Howard Finster Man of Visions.* New York City, 1989. (Contains extensive bibliography.)

## JAMES HAROLD JENNINGS

b. 1931

*Aeon-Angel-Metempsychosis*

1988, signed and inscribed verso
Polychromed plywood, 22 x 21 inches
1990.137

Born, Pinnacle, North Carolina; received minimal education in King, North Carolina; began to paint in 1974; active in Pinnacle.

Jennings lives and works in a site-specific environment he has created from a number of buses and log structures. This environment is enhanced by the presence of cutouts of various animals and angels, all designed with a strong, clean, well-rounded sense of line, softly and warmly colored. Like many visionaries, Jennings lives by a personal code of transcendence with rather elaborate extended metaphors. The angel "Aeon" is the embodiment and herald of Jennings' faith in metempsychosis.

### PROVENANCE
From the artist to the collection of Anne and Howard Smith, Martinsville, Virginia; to American Primitive Gallery, New York City; by purchase to Southeastern Newspapers Corporation; by gift to Morris Museum of Art.

### LITERATURE
Manley, Roger. *Signs and Wonders: Outsider Art Inside North Carolina.* Raleigh, North Carolina Museum of Art, Raleigh, 1989.

Mhire, Herman, Andy Nacisse, and Maude Southwell Wahlman. *Baking in the Sun: Visionary Images from the South.* University of Southwestern Louisiana Art Museum, Lafayette, 1987.

Perryman, Thomas R. and Howard A. and Anne Smith. *Fine Folk: Art'n'Facts From the Rural South.* Martinsville, Virginia, Piedmont Arts Association, 1990.

Rosenak, Chuck and Jan. *Museum of American Folk Art Encyclopedia of Twentieth-Century American Folk Art and Artists.* New York City, 1990.

### EXHIBITION HISTORY
"Fine Folk: Art'n'Facts From the Rural South," Piedmont Arts Association, Martinsville, Virginia, November 17, 1989-January 7, 1990, Roanoke Museum of Fine Arts, Roanoke, Virginia, June 14, 1990-September 9, 1990, American Primitive Gallery, New York City, November 1, 1990-December 1, 1990.

BENJAMIN (B.F.) PERKINS

b. 1904

*Cherokee Love Birds*

Signed lower right
Oil on plywood, 48 x 29 inches
1992.013

Born, Vernon, Alabama; took some art courses at Albert Brewer Junior College, Fayette, Alabama; began to paint in 1979; active in Bankston, Alabama.

Most of Perkins' art is concerned with expressing his personal belief in God and country. His art takes the form of signs, with extensive messages recounting his experiences as a minister or his revelation of the pathway to salvation through repentance, prayer, and belief. As Anne Smith notes, his paintings of birds "are perhaps the only exceptions to his favorite patriotic/religious theme" and often depict "colorful peacock-like tails." Repetitive, recursive lines are frequent manifestations in the self-taught idiom. The combination of strong color and recurring form in this particular work has a slightly dizzy effect, enhanced by the rather large scale.

**PROVENANCE**
From the artist to Ghislane Vander Elst; by purchase to Morris Museum of Art.

**LITERATURE**
Perryman, Thomas R. and Howard A. and Anne Smith. *Fine Folk: Art'n'Facts From the Rural South.* Piedmont Arts Association, Martinsville, Virginia, 1990.

Rosenak, Chuck and Jan. *Museum of American Folk Art Encyclopedia of Twentieth-Century American Folk Art and Artists.* New York City, 1990.

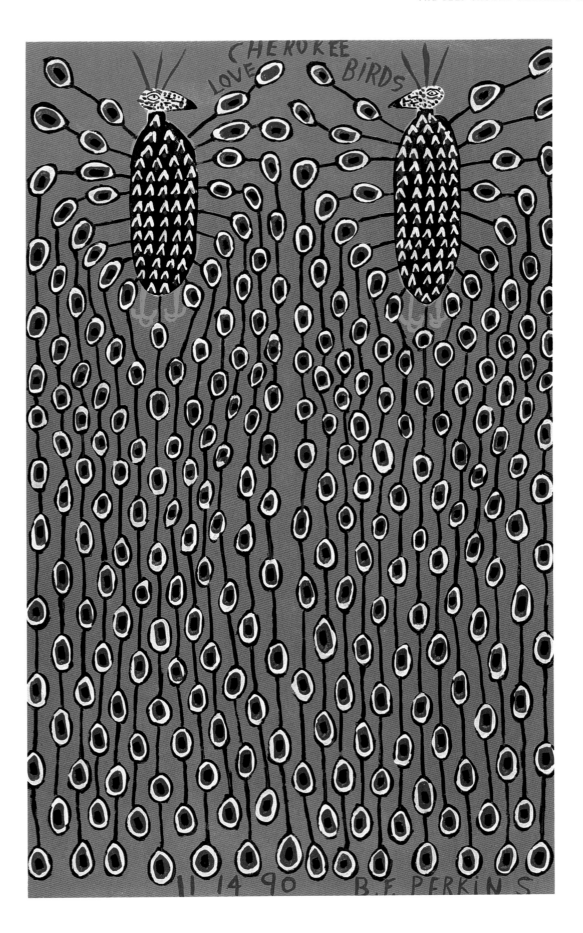

## JIMMY LEE SUDDUTH

b. 1910

Born, Caines Ridge, Alabama; minimal education; claims to have made mud paintings since he was three years old, but first exhibited publicly in the late 1960s; active in Fayette, Alabama.

*Self-Portrait*

Signed upper left
Tempera on plywood, 48 x 24 inches
1991.005

Many of Sudduth's first works were created with mud mixed with sugar water, a combination the artist felt gave them permanency and hardness. His figures are bold, close to the picture plane, and drawn with a deceptively simple sense of line. The character that emerges from this self-portrait seems to have a wary self-confidence and a halting regard for the violating stare of the viewer.

PROVENANCE
From the artist to Red Piano Gallery, Hilton Head, South Carolina; by purchase to Southeastern Newspapers Corporation; by gift to Morris Museum of Art.

LITERATURE
Museum of York County. *Living Traditions: Southern Black Folk Art*. Rock Hill, South Carolina, 1991.

Rosenak, Chuck and Jan. *Museum of American Folk Art Encyclopedia of Twentieth-Century American Folk Art and Artists*. New York City, 1990.

# Contemporary Southern Painting

Without straining the point, it might be possible to see contemporary painting in the South perpetuating those narrative concerns that arose during the cultural renascence of the '20s. While it is true that individuals of genius – notably Will Henry Stevens, Paul Ninas, Ida Kohlmeyer, and Lamar Dodd – created works in the abstract style, they neither followed nor inspired followers to any large extent.

On the other hand, those same Southern grotesque fantasies one experiences in John McCrady and Robert Gwathmey earlier in the century abound in many current works. The South, itself, and the many delicious layers of Southern social life and manners, continue to inform a vast array of artists of considerable talent.

It may be that the traditions of painting must take root and mature in a culture over sufficient length of time to afford proper perspective upon past and present. From that view it would seem, at the moment, that modernism and abstraction on the national scale are intellectually bankrupt, and, hence, the alarming sham of a "post-modern" era.

However, painting in the South is alive as never before. An extremely vital school of artists in New Orleans continues to produce a body of work that does not seek to provoke in order to express. Furthermore, many artists with Southern backgrounds now living outside the South, like Roger Brown, are finding a wealth of subject matter from their heritage.

# ROBERT GORDY

1933-1986

Born, Jefferson Island, Louisiana; M.F.A., Louisiana State University; active in New Orleans; died, New Orleans.

## *The Scylla and Charybdis Factor*

1970, signed and dated lower right
Acrylic on canvas, 61 x 69 inches
1990.112

Robert Gordy was an enormously complex artist who brought a well-honed, art-historical, intellectual sensibility to his painting. As a young man he was deeply influenced by the drawings of Nicolas Poussin and a particular work of Cezanne, titled *The Bathers*. What Gordy seems to have admired in these works was the bare bones of their composition, the simple line drawings that provided the foundation for fleshing out an extended narrative.

From this appreciation, Gordy developed a uniquely personal style, which seems somewhat akin to the Chicago imagism of Roger Brown, and looks ahead to the bold figurative drawings of Keith Haring. Gordy's style might be called hard-edged figurative painting. He painted large, contoured figures that were often drawn with a recurrent, or reappearing, line, arranged repetitively in polite, conforming rows. Dense, patterned, often erotic, they display a smooth control of paint, indeed, an exhausting technical finesse, which Gordy came to call "knitting."

After his successful retrospective of 1981, however, Gordy abandoned this demanding form for the more expressionistic technique of monotype. A series of large heads, some of horrific proportions, ensued. *The Scylla and Charybdis Factor* is a reference to the classic myth of the two floating towers of stone that beset Ulysses on his odyssey. Tinged with subliminal eroticism, they suggest the loss of individuality in the tumultuous tides of orgiastic sexuality. Gordy's death, at 52, robbed the Southern art world of one of the towering figures of the age, perhaps the most truly original and creative Southern painter in the twentieth century.

### PROVENANCE
From the artist to the collection of Russell Albright and Michael Myers, New Orleans; by gift to the New Orleans Museum of Art to benefit the 1990 Odyssey Ball; by purchase to Southeastern Newspapers Corporation; by gift to Morris Museum of Art.

### LITERATURE
Adams, Franklin. "An Interview with Robert Gordy." *Les Beaux Arts.* News Orleans, c. 1985.

Baro, Gene. *Robert Gordy: Paintings and Drawings: 1960-1980.* New Orleans Museum of Art, 1981. (Contains extensive bibliography.)

Kramer, Hilton. "Images, Patterns and the Mainstream." *The New York Times,* May 9, 1980.

Pennington, Estill Curtis. *A New Quarter: Contemporary New Orleans Artists.* Lauren Rogers Museum of Art, Laurel, Mississippi,1983.

Schwartzman, Allan, and Kathleen Thomas, and Marchia Tucker. *The 1970s, New American Painting.* The New Museum, New York City, 1979.

Virginia Museum. *Painting in the South: 1564-1980.* Richmond, 1983.

Walker, Barry. *Robert Gordy.* University of South Florida Galleries. Tampa, 1985.

### ARCHIVAL SOURCES
Archives of American Art, Smithsonian Institution. (See Mitchell Kahn's oral history with the artist.)
New Orleans Museum of Art, curatorial files.
Ogden Collection, New Orleans, curatorial files.

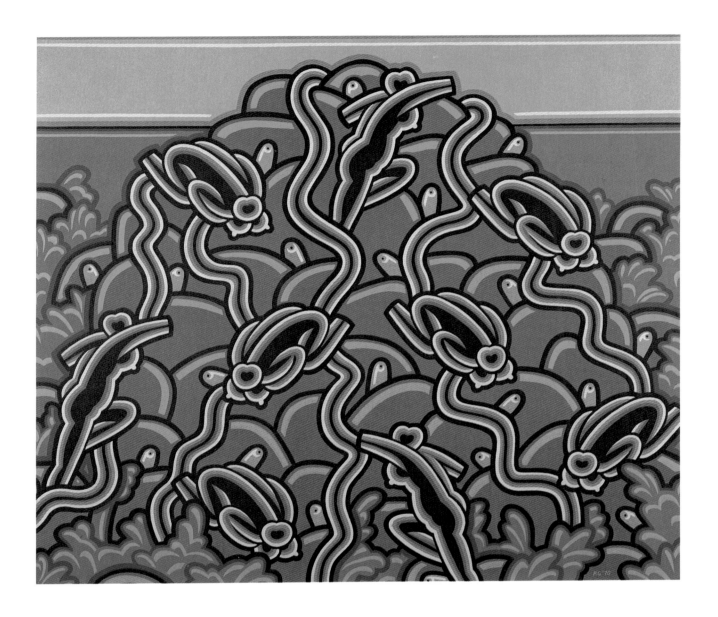

# IDA KOHLMEYER

b. 1912

Born, New Orleans; M.F.A., Sophie Newcomb Art School of Tulane University; also studied with John McCrady, George Rickey, Pat Trivigno, Mark Rothko, and Hans Hofmann; active in Metairie, Louisiana, and New Orleans.

## Mythic Series #5

1984, signed and dated lower middle
Mixed media on canvas, 59½ x 49½ inches
1990.098

Ida Kohlmeyer has always balanced a cultivated awareness of prevailing modernist trends with an almost relentless pursuit of excellence in her own art. As a young painter, she was deeply influenced by Hans Hofmann, the result being a series of works with a strong abstract composition. In the late 1950s, her concerns turned toward color field painting, and it is really as a superb colorist that she should be best known. During the late '50s and early '60s she was influenced by Mark Rothko, an influence compounded by study with that artist during his stay at Tulane. From that point a nascent, transcendental spirit enters her works, giving them, in the best abstract tradition, a suggestive spirituality.

Since the early '70s, Kohlmeyer has worked in a mode reminiscent of Adolph Gottlieb's pictographic style. These works, while abstract, often split the picture plane into compartments in which colorful semiotic elements compete for attention. *Mythic Series #5* is another in the series of works that Kohlmeyer has painted to spark an atavistic response to the redeeming, mystic power of nature. It is this power which Whitney Engeran, in the Mint Museum catalog, calls "the sacred atmosphere of wholeness and plenitude in human living" (p. 46).

**PROVENANCE**
From the artist to Arthur Roger Gallery, New Orleans; by purchase to Southeastern Newspapers Corporation; by gift to Morris Museum of Art.

**LITERATURE**
Frank, Peter. *Ida Kohlmeyer, Painting and Sculpture*. Arthur Roger Gallery, New Orleans, 1989.

Kohlmeyer, Ida. "About Rothko." *Arts Quarterly*. New Orleans Museum of Art, 1982.

Mint Museum of Art. *Ida Kohlmeyer: Thirty Years*. Charlotte, North Carolina, 1983. (Contains extensive bibliography.)

# EDWARD RICE

b. 1953

## *Dormer*

1984-87, signed and dated lower right
Oil on canvas, 48 x 48 inches
1990.092

Born, Augusta, Georgia; studied with Freeman Schoolcraft, Augusta; active in Augusta.

While it is tempting to consider Ed Rice's art as a manifestation of the photo-realistic reaction to avant-garde art movements of the 1960s, it actually reflects a far greater discipline. Rice described the process of his method to Lynn Myers in 1988: "First I do a quick sketch of the idea, and then I make approximately 100 photographs .... From the photographs I work as a draftsman so I have a very accurate, geometrically constructed drawing on the canvas."

*Dormer* is enhanced by the square format and the coloration, which reeks of the deep South. It projects outward with a geometric accuracy that almost defies the restraining shield of the picture plane. As such, it makes an interesting comparison to the expressive on-site works of an artist like Elemore Morgan, even as it gives a very finite sense of one very specific aspect of place.

**PROVENANCE**
From the artist to Donna Jaffe Fishbein, Providence, Rhode Island; to Heath Gallery, Atlanta; by purchase to Southeastern Newspapers Corporation; by gift to Morris Museum of Art.

**LITERATURE**
Claussen, Keith. "Personal Vision." *Augusta Magazine* (May/June 1987).

Lieberman, Laura. "The Southern Artist: Ed Rice." *Southern Accents* (March/April 1987).

Meyer, Jon. *Edward Rice: Tree Paintings.* The Heath Gallery, Atlanta, 1990. (Contains extensive bibliography.)

Morrin, Peter and Lynn Robertson Myers. *Edward Rice: Paintings and Drawings.* McKissick Museum, Columbia, South Carolina, 1987.

Schoolcraft, Faye. "Edward Rice." *Art Voices South* (March/April 1980).

**EXHIBITION HISTORY**
"Edward Rice: Paintings and Drawings," McKissick Museum, University of South Carolina, Columbia, May 7-June 14, 1987.

# ELEMORE MORGAN, JR.

b. 1931

## *Early Homesite*

1985, signed lower right
Acrylic on canvas, 26 x 54¼ inches
1990.107

Born, Baton Rouge, Louisiana; B.F.A., Louisiana State University, C.F.A., Ruskin School of Fine Arts, Oxford, England; active in Lafayette, Louisiana.

Like the first French impressionists, Morgan often works *en plein air,* or out-of-doors, in his native Louisiana, painting the glories of the countryside he loves so well. "In recent years," he told Mike Maher, "what I feel I'm doing is looking at this so-called horizon and the clouds above it, and thinking that I'm seeing a thin slice of the planet. I realize that these things we call sunrise and sunset result from the Earth's movement, and the interaction of sunlight with the atmosphere. I can almost sense my place on the planet and feel the curvature and the movement of the Earth."

Morgan's results have tremendous spontaneity. His palette, while bright, is greatly enhanced by his superb brushwork, strokes that can suggest the pace of a cloud as it moves across the sky, or the imminence of rain. All of these effects he reproduces on shaped panels of masonite. "Rectangles seem abrupt to me," he commented in the same article. "Shaped panels are more encompassing. I find them an integral part of the image; they heighten the space-form relationships."

**PROVENANCE**
From the artist to Arthur Roger Gallery, New Orleans; by purchase to Southeastern Newspapers Corporation; by gift to Morris Museum of Art.

**LITERATURE**
Harlan, Calvin. *Elemore Morgan, Jr. Paintings, Drawings, Photographs 1953-1981.* Natural History Museum, Lafayette, Louisiana,1982. (Contains extensive bibliography.)
Maher, Mike. "Direct Observations of Elemore Morgan, Jr." *La Louisiane* (Spring 1990).

## GEORGE DUREAU

b. 1930

*Rehearsal in Ring Number 1*

1987-88, signed lower left
Oil on canvas, 89 x 68 inches
1990.104

Born, New Orleans; B.F.A., Louisiana State University, Baton Rouge; active in New Orleans.

Although Dureau is a legendary photographer whose grotesque, and often homo-erotic, images inspired a legion of imitators, Robert Mapplethorpe not the least among them, his personal quest has been to achieve perfection in the realm of figurative drawing and painting. Even as the critical debate swirls around him as to whether he is a neo-classic artist or a throwback to the German romantics, he placidly pursues the figure from life in his studio in the French Quarter.

Regardless of how one considers Dureau's art, his formal concerns are more than obvious. He continues to tackle the difficult problem of placing, modeling, contouring, and invigorating the translation of the figure from a live, three-dimensional model to a captivating two-dimensional vision. That he is successful is due, in part, to his superb natural talents as a draftsman, and in even larger part to his passionate regard for the figure itself. To this eye, there is always something of the Baroque to Dureau's art. The painting at hand has far more in common with the defiance of the picture plane by the mannerists, especially in the curvilinear manner in which these figures seem to pierce the space behind them, than it has in common with the cool, rather repressed longings of the neo-classics to realize human form in its most perfect state.

**PROVENANCE**
From the artist to Arthur Roger Gallery, New Orleans; by purchase to Southeastern Newspapers Corporation; by gift to Morris Museum of Art.

**LITERATURE**
Calas, Terrington. "George Dureau: The Modern Heroic Figure." *New Orleans Art Review* (1988).

Contemporary Arts Center. *George Dureau: Selected Works 1960-1977*. New Orleans, 1977.

Davis, Melody. *The Male Nude in Contemporary Photography*. Philadelphia, 1991.

Lucie-Smith, Edward. *Art in the Eighties*. London, England, 1990.

———. "George Dureau: Classical/Anti-Classical?" *New Orleans Art Review* (1983).

Pennington, Estill Curtis. *Look Away: Reality and Sentiment in Southern Art*. Atlanta, 1989.

**ARCHIVAL SOURCES**
Historic New Orleans Collection.

New Orleans Museum of Art.

## DAVID BATES

b. 1952

Born, Dallas, Texas; M.F.A., Southern Methodist University, Dallas; active in Texas.

### *Mullet and Shells*

1990, signed lower right
Oil on canvas, 32 x 44 inches
1990.097

David Bates' paintings often depict the more sporting aspects of the lingering wilderness landscape of the rural South. His settings are the remote swamps, creeks, and bayous of East Texas, with the occasional evocation of classic Louisiana scenes in the spirit of Meeker and Buck. When these scenes are inhabited, one gazes upon the large, gawky figures of the Southern grotesque, composed with a slightly leering sense of line that renders them in a cartoonish fashion, though not as unpleasant caricatures. It is this sense of line that gives Bates' work such powerful immediacy. Like works by other artists in this collection, notably Don Cooper and Douglas Bourgeois, they tread the line of magic realism, with images so commanding and so recognizable, yet captured in so fantastic a manner as to unsettle even as they send out a familiar greeting. *Mullet and Shells* has all the familiar reference of a Southern still life composed from elements at hand. At the same time, curiously enough, the subdued palette and color harmonics remind one of the work of the artist Marsden Hartley in New England.

**PROVENANCE**
From the artist to the Arthur Roger Gallery, New Orleans; by purchase to Southeastern Newspapers Corporation; by gift to Morris Museum of Art.

**LITERATURE**
Charles Cowles Gallery. *David Bates.* New York City, 1988. (Contains extensive bibliography.)

## WILLIAM J. PETRIE

b. 1951

Born, Grant County, Kentucky; B.F.A., Northern Kentucky Community College; active in Grant County and Lexington, Kentucky.

### *Dog Thief*

1989, signed upper right
Acrylic on canvas, 24 x 20 inches
1990.016

Bill Petrie's paintings often tell delightfully fantastic stories. With a broad brush that combines kinetic cartoonish figures leaping about in wild abandon with the clear curves of well-constructed anatomical forms, they evoke that warmth and humor that comes from the human comedy. *Dog Thief* is "Lassie Come Home" gone bad. Even as the angry owners in the background scream obscenities at the fleeing figure, who recalls Adonis more than a dark villain, the happy dog stares out from the picture plane with an air of contentment. More than any other mood, the painting conveys energy and motion, and the delirious thrill of the chase.

**PROVENANCE**
From the artist by purchase to Southeastern Newspapers Corporation; by gift to Morris Museum of Art.

## DOUGLAS BOURGEOIS

b. 1951

### *The Suitcase*

1990, signed lower right
Oil on panel, 16 x 20 inches
1990.101

Born, Gonzales, Louisiana; B.F.A. , Louisiana State University, Baton Rouge; active in Gonzales and New Orleans.

New Orleans critics Roger Green and Eric Bookhardt see the art of Douglas Bourgeois as part of a distinct Louisiana movement Bookhardt has termed "visionary imagists." These artists, Green has written, "work in a tight, polished figurative style, usually with a palette of jewel-bright colors. All express mystical sensibilities, usually related to topical issues and ideals. Moral concerns often are cloaked in absurdist humor." In Bourgeois' work the exalted and the commonplace exist side-by-side. *The Suitcase* has the air of transformation one associates with Ovidian metamorphosis. Butterflies burst forth in a scene of pollution and decay, even as the beautiful lovers embrace. This love among the ruins is hardly pornographic; indeed, it is a vision of loveliness even if the bleach bottles are rather prominently strewn about the remains of suburban domestic splendor.

According to Green, Bourgeois, "the most conventionally spiritual of the Visionary Imagists, equates the lives of the saints with those of music and movie stars. 'Both', he has said, 'are searching for some higher kind of satisfaction ... a way to transcend ordinariness.'" Throughout Bourgeois' work Green sees those in need "being healed by beneficent nature." Here there is the rather extended suggestion that we do indeed bring our own baggage to the surroundings in which we seek that transcendence. *The Suitcase* is a parable of modern life, in which the mundane and the spiritual compete on equal terms, if not toward similar ends.

PROVENANCE
From the artist to Arthur Roger Gallery, New Orleans; by purchase to Southeastern Newspapers Corporation; by gift to Morris Museum of Art.

LITERATURE
Green, Roger. "Powerful Messages from the Visionary Imagists." *New Orleans Times-Picayune Lagniappe,* January 4, 1991.

Pennington, Estill Curtis. *A New Quarter: Contemporary New Orleans Artists.* Lauren Rogers Museum of Art, Laurel, Mississippi, 1983.

Southeastern Center for Contemporary Art. *Awards in the Visual Arts I.* Winston-Salem, North Carolina, 1982.

## ROGER BROWN

b. 1942

*Hurricane Hugo*

1990
Oil on canvas, 48 x 72 inches
1990.103

Born, Opelika, Alabama; M.F.A., School of the Art Institute, Chicago, 1970; active in Chicago, but makes periodic trips to Alabama.

At first glance, Roger Brown's paintings appear to be deceptively simple cartoons in which familiar episodes from history, or the recent past, are spiffed up in bright colors and set down before the viewer in an arresting freeze-frame. As one of the masters of the Chicago Imagist School, Brown was a pioneer in leading contemporary art of the 1970s away from the obscure meanings of abstraction and toward new levels of representational allusion.

Though he has functioned in Chicago for a number of years, he continues to credit his Southern past for inspiration in his work. In an interview with Phyllis Kind and Ray Yoshida published in the Lawrence volume, Brown acknowledges the South, by way of responding to country music. "When I first came away from the South to Chicago I couldn't stand it. Then ... I realized I could identify with it. It's satire, it's about vernacular, it always tells simple stories. I realized how much it was like what I'm doing."

Like other Southern writers and artists, Brown has seen the potential for expression in the humorous, absurd, even grotesque side of Southern culture. This ability to turn tragedy to comedy is at work in *Hurricane Hugo,* where the full fury of nature has worked so evenly to lop off the Carolina palms and pines at exactly the same level. As the great leveler, nature spares no one. Brown has turned the entire episode into a gigantic postcard from the 1950s, luridly colored and humiliatingly equitable.

**PROVENANCE**
From the artist to Arthur Roger Gallery, New Orleans; by purchase to Southeastern Newspapers Corporation; by gift to Morris Museum of Art.

**LITERATURE**
Lawrence, Sidney. *Roger Brown.* New York City, 1987. (Contains extensive bibliography.)

# DON COOPER

b. 1944

## *Extreme Southeast Georgia*

1990, signed verso
Oil on canvas, 60 x 70 inches
1992.011

Born, Madison, Georgia; M.F.A., University of Georgia; active in Atlanta.

Cooper's work over the past decade has often traced a path between experimental form and experimental content. He has created painted sculptural forms, and he has painted canvases with a tantalizingly elusive narrative content. In many of his paintings, there is the suggestion of nature under violent assault, a violence rendered more threatening by the use of intense color. *Extreme Southeast Georgia* is from a series of works in which Cooper infuses the Southern landscape with mythic elements from the Orient. This work was inspired by a visit to the grounds and gardens of the old Carnegie estate on Cumberland Island. A work of tremendous depth and visual seduction, it celebrates the natural supernaturalism of a landscape in decay, a traditional Southern theme.

**PROVENANCE**
From the artist to Phyllis Weil Gallery, New York City; by purchase to Morris Museum of Art.

**LITERATURE**
Cullen, J.W. "Art & Nature: Revisions of a Theme." *Art Papers* (November-December 1987).

Kipnis, Jeff. "Don Cooper." *Art Voices* (May-June 1981).

Lieberman, Laura C. "Honoring American Artists: SECCA'S Two Award Programs." *Southern Accents* 10, no. 2 (April 1987).

Pennington, Estill Curtis. "Don Cooper." Phyllis Weil Gallery exhibition brochure essay, 1991.

Yau, John. "Don Cooper at Phyllis Weil." *Art Forum* 26, no. 2 (October 1987).

**ARCHIVAL SOURCES**
Center for the Study of Southern Painting, Morris Museum of Art, Oral History Collection.

**EXHIBITION HISTORY**
"Don Cooper: Paintings and Sculptures," The Columbus Museum, Columbus, Georgia, May 11-September 11, 1992.

# FRANCIS X. PAVY

b. 1954

Born, Lafayette, Louisiana; B.F.A., University of Southwestern Louisiana, Lafayette; active in Lafayette.

## *Betting Money on the Cockfight*

1990, signed lower right
Oil on canvas, 37 x 37 inches
1990.109

Subliminal Cajun energies suffuse Pavy's work. A syncopated application of paint evokes the rhythms of zydeco music and lends an air of the exotic. But as with all deep South culture, there is also a threatening air, compounded by the bloody theme and the presence of that corrupting symbol, the dollar sign.

**PROVENANCE**
From the artist to Arthur Roger Gallery, New Orleans; by purchase to Southeastern Newspapers Corporation; by gift to Morris Museum of Art.

# JIM RICHARD

b. 1943

Born, Port Arthur, Texas; M.F.A., University of Colorado, Boulder; active in New Orleans.

## *Owning Modern Sculpture XXVI*

1991, signed and dated verso
Acrylic on canvas, 55 x 44¼ inches
1992.028

Richard's paintings are characterized by extremely odd juxtapositions. He re-creates interior spaces in colors that seem to have been refined by a gigantic commercial screen of the type used to break down colors for mechanical reproductive purposes. His attention to detail ensures that we are aware of each minute item in the room … rooms that often evoke the plastic spirit of the suburban South. In the midst of these rooms one often finds an ill-placed, indeed, entirely out-of-place piece of modern sculpture, looking as though it had been beamed down from a passing starship to the wrong coordinates. It is unexpected. While the sculpture does not belong there, it does have the same coloration, and seems to blend quite nicely with the surroundings even if it doesn't fit in. Could this be right?

**PROVENANCE**
From the artist to Arthur Roger Gallery, New York City; by purchase to Morris Museum of Art.

**LITERATURE**
Hughes, Robert. "Art: Quirks, Clamors, and Variety." *Time* magazine (March 2, 1981).
Pennington, Estill Curtis. *A New Quarter: Contemporary New Orleans Artists.* Lauren Rogers Museum of Art, Laurel, Mississippi, 1983.
Russell, John. "A Roundup of Emerging Artists." *The New York Times,* February 8, 1981.

# Checklist of the Permanent Southern Collection

**JOHN ABBOT**
*Gold Bird*
  Watercolor on hand-laid
  off-white paper
  11⅛ x 8¾ inches
  1981.B-009

*Yellow Breasted Finch*
  Watercolor on hand-laid
  off-white paper
  11⅛ x 8¾ inches
  1981.B-004

*Natural History of Rarer
Lepidopterous Insects of Georgia*
  Hand-colored plates
  16¼ x 13 x 1½ inches
  M-1989.H

*Forked Tail Hawk*
  Watercolor on hand-laid
  off-white paper
  11⅛ x 8¾ inches
  1981.B-010

*Great Brown Hawk*
  Watercolor on hand-laid
  off-white paper
  11⅛ x 8¾ inches
  1981.B-007

*Plover, or Kildee*
  Watercolor on hand-laid
  off-white paper
  11⅛ x 8¾ inches
  1981.B-002

*Little Horn Owl or Screech Owl*
  Watercolor on hand-laid
  off-white paper
  11⅛ x 8¾ inches
  1981.B-006

*Yellow Spotted Headed Sparrow*
  Watercolor on hand-laid
  off-white paper
  11⅛ x 8¾ inches
  1981.B-001

*Purple Swallow*
  Watercolor on hand-laid
  off-white paper
  11⅛ x 8¾ inches
  1981.B-005

*Pale Yellow Throat*
  Watercolor on hand-laid
  off-white paper
  11⅛ x 8¾ inches
  1981.B-003

*Grebe, Didapper, or Water Witch*
  Watercolor on hand-laid
  off-white paper
  11⅛ x 8¾ inches
  1981.B-008

**WAYMAN ADAMS**
*New Orleans Mammy*
  Oil on canvas, 50 x 40 inches
  1989.01.001

**ENRIQUE ALFEREZ**
*Sophie B. Wright Monument*
  Graphite on paper, 28½ x 21¾ inches
  1992.005

**STEPHEN ALKE**
*Tobacco Setters on a Hilltop*
  Oil on canvas, 23¼ x 29⅛ inches
  1991.001

**WALTER INGLIS ANDERSON**
*Cabbages*
  Watercolor on paper
  25 x 19 inches
  1990.003

*Fall Pin Oaks with Birds*
  Watercolor on paper
  25 x 19 inches
  1990.001

*From Paradise Lost #47*
  Watercolor on paper
  25 x 19 inches
  1990.004

**Z. B. ARMSTRONG**
*Box with Cups, Year of 1986*
  Painted wood construction
  12½ x 10 inches
  1991.011

*Calendar 2*
  Felt marker on cardboard
  9⅛ x 11⅛ inches
  1991.010

*Calendar*
  Felt marker on cardboard
  11½ x 5¼ inches
  1991.009

**JOHN JAMES AUDUBON**
*Carolina Parakeet*
  Aquatint engraving on paper, (Havell)
  33 x 24 inches
  1989.02.234

**MAYNA TREANOR AVENT**
*The Powers Children,
Greenville, South Carolina*
  Watercolor on paper, 15⅝ x 12 inches
  1989.01.009

**A. E. BACKUS**
*Swamp Rigolets*
  Oil on canvas, 25 x 30 inches
  1989.07.276

**DAVID BATES**
*Rockport*
  Oil on canvas, 36 x 24 inches
  1990.096

*Mullet and Shells*
  Oil on canvas, 32 x 44 inches
  1990.097

**HILDA BELCHER**
*Run Little Chillun, Run, Fo'
De Devil's Done Loose...*
  Oil on board, 13⅞ x 11¾ inches
  1989.01.010

**BESSIE BELL**
*Plate of Strawberries, Quince
and Basket*
  Oil on canvas, 18 x 22 inches
  1989.01.011

**WENONAH DAY BELL**
*Greenville, Georgia*
  Watercolor on paper
  17¼ x 24 inches
  1989.01.012

*Table Top Still Life*
  Oil on canvas mounted on board
  18 x 20 inches
  1989.01.014

**SISTER AGNES BERCHMANS**
*The Christian Martyr, 1919*
  Oil on canvas, 22 x 42 inches
  1989.01.015

*Saint Cecilia*
  Oil on canvas, 23½ x 42¼ inches
  1989.01.016

**LOUIS L. BETTS**
*The Yellow Parasol*
  Oil on canvas, 50 x 40 inches
  1991.003

**JEANETTE KENNEY BLAIR**
*Conversation, Anniston,
Alabama, 1944*
  Watercolor and graphite on paper
  31 x 22½ inches
  1989.01.017

*Going on a Picnic, Anniston,
Alabama, 1944*
  Watercolor and graphite on paper
  31 x 22½ inches
  1989.01.018

**CHARLES L. BOISSET**
*Morning in Audubon Park,
New Orleans, La.*
  Oil on canvasboard
  16 x 12 inches
  1989.01.019

**DOUGLAS BOURGEOIS**
*Ball of Confusion*
  Mixed media construction
  17¾ x 12 inches
  1992.009

*Teensy, Noonie*
  Oil on canvas, 12 x 12 inches
  1992.006

*The Suitcase*
  Oil on panel, 16 x 20 inches
  1990.101

*Pure Spirit - Double Superfine*
  Oil and cut-out, collaged metal on
  wood, 8¾ x 6¾ x 1¾ inches
  1990.102

**CARL CHRISTIAN BRENNER**
*Beech Trees - Kentucky*
  Oil on canvas, 18 x 24¼ inches
  1989.01.020

**RALPH W. BREWER**
*Blowing Trees*
  Oil on board, 11¼ x 22 inches
  1989.08.286

**ALEXANDER BROOK**
*Church in South Carolina*
  Oil on canvas, 18 x 26 inches
  1989.01.021

*Savannah Street Scene*
  Pencil on paper, 10 x 15⅝ inches
  1990.062

**ROGER BROWN**
*Hurricane Hugo*
  Oil on canvas, 48 x 72 inches
  1990.103

**CHARLES EPHRAIM
BURCHFIELD**
*Early Night*
  Pencil on paper, 8¼ x 5 inches
  1989.01.023

*Guard House*
  Pencil on paper, 8¼ x 5 inches
  1989.01.022

*Tents at Twilight*
  Pencil on paper, 6¾ x 8¼ inches
  1989.01.024

**BUZZ BUSBY**
*Buzz Fan*
  Mixed media, 13 x 9 inches
  1990.131

**LYELL E. CARR**
*Opossum Snout, Haralson
County, Georgia*
  Oil on canvas, 28½ x 40½ inches
  1989.01.025

*The Shepherdess,
Haralson County, Georgia*
  Oil on canvas, 20 x 26 inches
  1989.01.026

**CAROLINE P. CARSON**
*Flowers*
  Watercolor on board, 10 x 8 inches
  1990.094

*Portrait of a Lady*
Watercolor on paper
13¼ x 10¼ inches
1989.01.027

WILLIE M. CHAMBERS
*Apples in a Straw Hat*
Oil on canvas, 17⅞ x 22⅛ inches
1989.01.029

*Basket of Cherries in a Landscape*
Oil on canvas, 13 x 18¼ inches
1989.01.030

*Basket of Peaches in a Landscape*
Oil on canvas, 15½ x 26 inches
1989.01.031

*Three Peaches in a Landscape*
Oil on board, 12 x 9 inches
1989.01.032

*Uncle Hamp and His Cart, Montezuma, Georgia*
Oil on canvas, 24 x 36 inches
1989.01.028

CONRAD WISE CHAPMAN
*Tidewater Creek in Evening Light*
Oil on canvas, 9 x 11 inches
1989.01.033

ELIOT CANDEE CLARK
*House in Snow - Virginia*
Oil on canvas, 26 x 26 inches
1989.01.034

*Savannah Harbor*
Oil on canvas, 20¼ x 24¼ inches
1990.028

JOHN CLEAVELAND
*Creek Bottom*
Oil on canvas, 24 x 37⅞ inches
1990.032

*Simple Answer*
Oil on canvas, 25 x 45⅞ inches
1990.031

ANN CADWALLADER COLES
*Portrait of a Man - Tack's Class*
Oil on canvas, 24 x 20 inches
1989.01.035

*Portrait of a Young Girl*
Oil on board, 16 x 20 inches
1989.01.036

AUGUST COOK
*Head of a Girl*
Oil on canvas, 13¾ x 9⅞ inches
1991.020

*Anne Greene*
Oil on canvas, 32¾ x 45 inches
1991.019

*Self-Portrait with Portrait*
Oil on canvas, 36 x 30 inches
1991.018

*Untitled (head of a woman)*
Oil on canvas, 20 x 16 inches
1991.021

IRMA COOK
*Untitled (woman with folded arms)*
Oil on canvas, 16 x 18 inches
1991.016

*Untitled (woman in red)*
Oil on canvas, 32 x 27 inches
1991.017

DON COOPER
*Extreme Southeast Georgia, 1990*
Oil on canvas, 60 x 70 inches
1992.011

*Perfumes of Ancient Times*
Oil on canvas, 66 x 77 inches
1990.065

GEORGE DAVID COULON
*Italian Capriccio*
Oil on canvas, 34 x 61 inches
1990.113

*Swamp Pools 1*
Oil on canvas, 36 x 18 inches
1989.07.277

*Swamp Pools 2*
Oil on canvas, 36 x 18 inches
1989.07.278

ELIZABETH E. CRAIG
*Memorabilia of General G. T. Anderson*
Oil on canvas, 36 x 27 inches
1989.01.037

JOSEPHINE M. CRAWFORD
*Nude*
Oil on masonite, 18⅞ x 13$^{3}/_{16}$ inches
1989.05.255

*Self-Portrait*
Oil on masonite, 15½ x 21 inches
1989.05.256

ELLIOTT DAINGERFIELD
*Carolina Sunlight*
Oil on canvas, 24 x 28¼ inches
1989.01.045

*Christ Stilling the Tempest*
Oil on canvas, 20 x 24 inches
1989.01.046

*Chrysanthemums in a Devil Vase*
Oil on canvas, 34 x 24 inches
1989.01.048

*The Genius of the Canyon*
Oil on canvas, 36 x 48½ inches
1989.01.039

*Golden Moon*
Oil on canvas, 6 x 8⅛ inches
1989.01.042

*Grandfather Mountain, N.C.*
Watercolor on paper, 9 x 12¼ inches
1989.01.044

*Head of a Mountain Woman*
Pencil on paper, 15 x 11 inches
1989.01.049

*Madonna and Child in Courtyard*
Oil on canvas, 12 x 20 inches
1989.01.040

*Milk Maid*
Oil on canvas, 24 x 34 inches
1989.01.041

*Mysterious Night*
Watercolor on board, 30½ x 21½ inches
1989.01.043

*The Mystic Brim*
Oil on canvas, 29¾ x 36 inches
1989.01.038

*Return at Twilight*
Oil on canvas, 28⅛ x 48⅛ inches
1989.01.047

*Steeplechase*
Oil on canvas, 7 x 9⅛ inches
1989.01.050

*Sunset Glory*
Oil on canvas, 27½ x 33¼ inches
1990.014

LAMAR DODD
*Bargain Basement*
Oil on canvas, 46 x 55 inches
1992.033

*11:15 P.M.*
Oil on canvas, 24 x 36 inches
1992.034

*Black Hull, 1986*
Watercolor on paper, 14⅛ x 20⅛ inches
1987.1.1

*Boats, 1986*
Watercolor on paper, 14⅛ x 20⅛ inches
1987.1.2

*From This Earth*
Oil on canvas, 24 x 39½ inches
1990.063

*Lobster Traps - Night No. 1, 1986*
Watercolor on paper, 18⅛ x 24 inches
1987.1.3

*Protective Harbor, 1986*
Watercolor on paper, 18⅛ x 24 inches
1987.1.4

WILLIAM de LEFTWICH DODGE
*Southern Pines*
Oil on canvas, 30¼ x 26 inches
1989.01.051

ALEXANDER JOHN DRYSDALE
*Bayou Landscape*
Kerosene-thinned oil on paper
19¼ x 29½ inches
1989.01.052

*Bayou By Moonlight*
Oil on board, 18½ x 24½ inches
1990.114

VICTOR DUBREUIL
*Cracking the Whip*
Oil on canvas, 16 x 20 inches
1990.115

GEORGE DUREAU
*Rehearsal in Ring Number 1*
Oil on canvas, 89 x 68 inches
1990.104

MINNIE EVANS
*Ark of the Covenant*
Oil, ink on canvasboard
14½ x 19½ inches
1990.008

*Creature in the Woods*
Colored crayon on paper
9 x 11½ inches
1990.005

*Untitled - Butterfly with Green Border*
Crayon, graphite, gold paint on paper
13½ x 11 inches
1990.006

*Untitled - Centaur with Two Figures*
Oil, pencil on paper backed canvas
12 x 9 inches
1990.009

*Untitled - Portrait with Stars*
Ink and gouache on paper, 12 x 9 inches
1990.007

HENRY FAULKNER
*Drawing on printed invitation*
Felt-tip pen on paper
7 x 4¾ inches
1991.012

*Still Life with Golden Slipper*
Oil on masonite, 16⅞ x 18⅞ inches
1990.064

HOWARD FINSTER
*Mona Lisa*
Oil paint on wood, 12½ x 7¼ x 4 inches
1990.078

EDWIN AUSTIN FORBES
*Defending a Battery - Confederate Cavalry Charge*
Pen and ink on paper, 10¾ x 14⅞ inches
1989.01.053

*The Mud March - Army of the Potomac*
Pen and ink on paper, 3⅞ x 7⅛ inches
1989.01.056

*A Tough Customer - Near Falmouth, Virginia*
Pen and ink on paper, 7¼ x 9⅝ inches
1989.01.055

*Writing It Up - Heroic Soldier of the Pen*
Pen and ink on paper, 4⅞ x 7¼ inches
1989.01.054

E.T.H. FOSTER
*Evening on the French Broad, N.C.*
Oil on canvas, 36½ x 54¾ inches
1989.03.235

TREVOR THOMAS FOWLER
*Willina S. Herndon*
Oil on canvas, 36 x 29 inches
1989.04.250

CHARLES FRASER
*Portrait of a Man*
Pencil and watercolor on paper
6½ x 5⅜ inches
1989.01.057

WILLIAM CARL ANTHONY FRERICHS
*Gorge, North Carolina*
Oil on canvas, 30 x 16¼ inches
1989.01.058

*Southern Mountain Landscape*
Oil on canvas, 32 x 47 inches
1989.01.059

*Waterfall, North Carolina*
Oil on canvas, 30 x 16 inches
1989.01.060

HENRY GASSER
*Dock at Georgetown, South Carolina*
Watercolor on paper, 14½ x 20½ inches
1989.01.061

WILLIAM GILBERT GAUL
*The Infantryman*
Watercolor on board, 16½ x 10 inches
1989.01.062

KAREKIN GOEKJIAN
*Reverend John D. Ruth, Woodville, Ga.*
Photograph, 15⅞ x 19⅞ inches
1992.032

WILLIAM O. GOLDING
*St. Yacht Ramona*
Crayon and pencil on paper
8¾ x 11¼ inches
1989.01.063

ANNE GOLDTHWAITE
*Ballerina c. 1900*
Oil on canvas, 29 x 23 inches
1989.01.064

*Two Girls*
Oil on canvas, 28¾ x 27 inches
1989.01.065

EMELINE H. GORDON
*Garden of the Earth - Owens-Thomas House, Savannah*
Oil on canvas, 18 x 16 inches
1989.01.066

ROBERT GORDY
*Wall No. 2*
Acrylic on canvas, 29½ x 46½ inches
1990.099

*The Scylla and Charybdis Factor*
Acrylic on canvas, 61 x 69 inches
1990.112

*Study for Landscape with Reclining Figure*
Marker, ink and colored pencil on paper
10½ x 11¼ inches
1992.001

*Untitled*
Acrylic on canvas, 26 x 24¼ inches
1990.100

ANGELA GREGORY
*Young Man Kneeling with Cigarette*
Sepia chalk on paper, 23¾ x 17¾ inches
1990.087

*Young Man in Shorts Leaning*
Sepia chalk on paper, 24 x 15½ inches
1990.086

*Young Man with a Pole*
Sepia chalk on paper, 27½ x 16¼ inches
1990.088

RENE GUERIN
*Oconee County Hay Bales*
Oil on canvas, 24 x 32 inches
1990.029

CAROLINE GUIGNARD
*Wash Day*
Pastel on paper, 7½ x 10¾ inches
1989.01.067

ROBERT GWATHMEY
*Reflections*
Oil on canvas, 26¾ x 32 inches
1992.024

ELLEN DAY HALE
*Cityscape from Park, Charleston, 1923*
Etching on paper, 6¼ x 4⅜ inches
1989.01.068

*Old Pines, North Carolina*
Etching on paper, 6⅞ x 4⅞ inches
1989.01.069

*Pecan Trees, Charleston, South Carolina*
Etching on paper, 6⅝ x 4¾ inches
1989.01.070

W. H. HARRINGTON
*Nature's Bounty*
Oil on board, 11½ x 17¼ inches
1990.116

RACHEL V. HARTLEY
*Church Meeting*
Oil on canvas, 25 x 30 inches
1989.01.072

*Mom Liza and her Children*
Oil on canvasboard, 20 x 24 inches
1989.01.071

T.A. HAY
*Old Charly*
Wood stain on wood, 8½ x 9⅛ inches
1990.082

*2 Birds, 2 Horses, Dog*
Wood stain on cardboard
12⅛ x 10⅛ inches
1990.084

*Horse*
Mixed media on wood, 5 x 6⅞ inches
1990.083

KNUTE HELDNER
*A Home on the Bayou*
Oil on canvas, 40 x 34 inches
1989.01.073

ELLA SOPHONISBA HERGESHEIMER
*Gladiolas in a Blue Vase*
Oil on canvas, 36 x 25 inches
1989.01.076

*Mountain Landscape - River Bridge*
Watercolor on paper, 10 x 13½ inches
1989.01.074

*Vase of Flowers, Drapery, Inkwell*
Oil on canvas, 21¾ x 25½ inches
1989.01.075

HERMAN HERZOG
*Florida Marsh*
Oil on canvas, 15⅝ x 20½ inches
1989.01.077

LOUISE LYONS HEUSTIS
*Portrait of a Lady*
Oil on canvas, 43½ x 38 inches
1989.01.078

GEORGE F. HIGGINS
*Florida Cabin Scene*
Oil on canvas, 12 x 18 inches
1989.01.079

*Palm Grove, Florida*
Oil on board, 13½x 19½ inches
1990.118

*Florida Landscape*
Oil on board, 9 x 17¼ inches
1990.117

NANCY L. HOEHN
*St. Luke's*
Oil on canvas, 18 x 20 inches
1990.026

LONNIE HOLLEY
*Eye Have the Hand that Holds the Staff for the Ancestors' Sake*
Watercolor, tempera on paper
22 x 28 inches
1990.129

NORA HOUSTON
*First Communion*
Oil on canvas, 28 x 34 inches
1989.01.081

*Portrait of the Gibson Children*
Oil on canvas, 20 x 24 inches
1989.01.080

WALTER TIREE HUDSON
*Abstracttus*
Acrylic and tempera on canvas
22 x 28 inches
1992.022

*Rainbow Over Dreamland*
Acrylic and tempera on canvas
22 x 28 inches
1992.020

*Errbius II*
Acrylic and tempera on canvas
22 x 28 inches
1992.019

*Oh It's Seribbleus*
Acrylic and tempera on canvas
22 x 28 inches
1992.021

MARIE ATKINSON HULL
*Blue Parrots, Florida*
Oil on canvas, 25⅛ x 25⅛ inches
1989.01.082

CLEMENTINE HUNTER
*Black Jesus*
Oil on board, 23½ x 8 7/16 inches
1990.024

ALFRED HEBER HUTTY
*Flower Vendor, Charleston, South Carolina*
Oil on canvas, 33¼ x 35½ inches
1989.01.084

*Guardian Oak*
Pencil on paper, 16 1/16 x 12¼ inches
1991.013

*Oxcart*
Pencil on paper, 3⅝ x 4½ inches
1989.01.086

*Oxcart and Cabin*
Pencil and ink wash on paper
3 15/16 x 5¾ inches
1989.01.083

*Voodoo Ritual*
Watercolor on paper
21¼ x 29⅞ inches
1989.01.085

HELEN HATCH INGLESBY
*Dr. Coggins*
Silhouette on paper, 5⅝ x 4½ inches
COG-XX17

*Front Porch Suitor (The Courting)*
Pastel on paper, 15⅝ x 19⅞ inches
1990.119

GEORGE INNESS JR.
*The Hunt*
Oil en grisaille on board
15¾ x 23¾ inches
1990.138

*Rainbow in Georgia*
Oil on canvas, 16 x 24 inches
1989.01.087

SARAH (SADIE) IRVINE
*Young Man with a Violin*
Pencil on paper, 10½ x 8½ inches
1990.090

JOHN BEAUFAIN IRVING
*Little Johnny Reb*
Oil on canvas, 18⅛ x 14 inches
1989.01.088

JOSEPH JACKSON
*Portrait of a Gentleman of the Woodfin Family*
Oil on canvas, 24⅛ x 19⅝ inches
1989.01.089

*Portrait of a Lady of the Woodfin Family*
Oil on canvas, 24¾ x 19⅝ inches
1989.01.090

JAMES HAROLD JENNINGS
*Aeon-Angel-Metempsychosis*
Painted wood, 33⅛ x 24⅝ x ¼ inches
1990.137

HARVEY JOINER
*Cherokee Park*
Oil on canvas, 12 x 18 inches
1989.04.251

*Wooded Landscape*
Oil on canvas, 28 x 40 inches
1989.08.287

MYRTLE JONES
*Quiet Harbor, Savannah, Georgia*
Oil on board, 16 x 20 inches
1989.01.091

NELL CHOATE JONES
*Court Day, Marietta*
Charcoal, pencil, ink and gouache on tracing paper, 19 x 24 inches
1989.01.096

*A Family Affair*
Mixed media on paper, 19½ x 26 inches
1989.01.092

*Georgia Red Clay*
Oil on canvas, 25 x 30 inches
1989.01.094

*Marietta Saturday*
Mixed media on paper, 16¼ x 22 inches
1989.01.097

*Spring Time - Flower Vendor Entering Atlanta*
Charcoal, pencil, ink and gouache on tracing paper, 13¾ x 20¼ inches
1989.01.093

*Watermelon Harvest*
Oil on canvas, 25 x 30 inches
1989.01.095

SUE JOY
*Mountain Farm, Tennessee*
Watercolor on paper, 14 x 21¼ inches
1989.01.099

SUSAN KEMPTON
*Texas Rainbow*
Oil on canvas, 48 x 72 inches
1990.067

CHARLEY KINNEY
*We Saw 7 Rainbows 7 Suns
This Day*
Watercolor on paper, 22 x 28½ inches
1990.080

*Loggers (with water snake)*
Watercolor on paper, 22 x 28½ inches
1990.079

ALBERTA KINSEY
*Portrait - Lady in Front of
Cotton Field*
Oil on canvas mounted on board
20 x 20½ inches
1989.01.100

IDA KOHLMEYER
*Medusa Chair*
Polychromed wooden chair
40 x 27 x 25 inches
1992.030

*Mythic Series No. 5*
Mixed media on canvas
59½ x 49½ inches
1990.098

GEORGE COCHRAN LAMBDIN
*Roses and Fuchsia*
Oil on board, 22 x 12 inches
1992.026

*Roses*
Oil on board, 22 x 14 inches
1992.025

RANDY LAMBETH
*Morning, King Mill*
Oil on canvas, 25 x 30 inches
1990.025

MELINDA MOORE LAMPKIN
*Feelin' Blue*
Collage, 13½ x 10½ inches
1990.020

GEORGE D. LEE
*Kentucky Landscape,
Near Louisville*
Oil on board, 12 x 10½ inches
1989.04.252

ADELE LEMM
*Gulls on the Beach*
Pastel on paper, 20 x 26½ inches
1989.01.102

*Harbor No. 9*
Pastel on paper, 18¾ x 23½ inches
1989.01.101

*Harbor Scene*
Pastel on paper, 20 x 26½ inches
1989.01.104

*Island Houses*
pastel on paper, 20⅛ x 26¼ inches
1989.01.103

JOSEPH CHRISTIAN
LEYDENDECKER
*Portrait of Rex Beach*
Oil on canvas board, 12 x 10 inches
1989.01.105

JOE L. LIGHT
*Ignorance is . . .*
House paint on wood, 33 x 21 inches
1992.016

*Good Information*
House paint on wood, 7 x 29 inches
1992.017

*People Don't Know*
House paint on wood, 8 x 28 inches
1992.018

FRANK B. LLOYD
*Playing Marbles*
Oil on board, 17¾ x 24 inches
1989.01.106

FRANK LONDON
*Tyranny of Survival*
Oil on canvas, 42 x 30 inches
1992.010

CHARLIE LUCAS
*The Peacock That Lost Its
Feathers*
Acrylic on plywood, with straw and
garden hose, 24 x 39⅜ inches
1990.132

JAMES P. LYLE
*Low Country - South Carolina*
Oil on linen, 50 x 70 inches
1992.031

HERMON ATKINS MACNEIL
*Christ Church near Charleston*
Oil on canvas, 36½ x 28¾ inches
1989.01.107

BLONDELLE MALONE
*Landscape - North Carolina*
Watercolor on paper, 9 x 13 inches
1989.01.108

ZELLE MANNING
*Clouds of Glory*
Acrylic on canvas, 24 x 36 inches
1992.003

*The Cross Leads Home*
Oil on canvas, 28 x 22 inches
1992.004

NICOLA MARSCHALL
*Portrait of Thomy King*
Oil on canvas, 36½ x 29 inches
1989.01.109

WILLIE MASSEY
*Peahen with Stars and Moon*
House paint on wood, 20 x 20½ inches
1990.136

FLORENCE LISTER LAND MAY
*Sailboat Beyond the Trees 1914*
Oil on canvas, 36 x 42 inches
1989.01.110

LAWRENCE MAZZONOVICH
*From Our Window, Fieldner's
Vineyard*
Oil on board, 18¾ x 26½ inches
1989.01.111

J. T. MCCORD
*Winged Alligator*
Acrylic on canvas, 16 x 20 inches
1991.007

*House with Fence*
Acrylic on canvas, 14 x 18 inches
1991.006

JOHN MCCRADY
*I Can't Sleep*
Oil on canvas, 35½ x 47½ inches
1989.05.260

*Louisiana Purchase*
Pencil on paper, 7¾ x 9¼ inches
1989.05.257

*Cartoon for 'Repatriated'*
Pencil on paper, 18¾ x 25¾ inches
1989.05.259

*Three Ages of Man*
Pencil on paper, 8 x 12¾ inches
1989.05.258

ALICE MCGEHEE
*Cabin in Spring*
Oil on canvas, 10⅛ x 14⅛ inches
1989.01.112

CARL MCKENZIE
*Kentucky Cardinal*
Carved wood, 4 x 8½ x 1½ inches
1990.074

*Avon Lady*
Carved wood, 17 x 4 x 3½ inches
1990.073

VIRGINIA RANDALL McLAWS
*Sycamores, Sweet Briar, Virginia*
Oil on canvas, 20⅛ x 16 inches
1989.01.114

*Texas Landscape*
Oil on board, 20 x 16 inches
1989.01.113

JOSEPH RUSLING MEEKER
*Bayou Landscape*
Oil on canvas, 18 x 27 inches
1990.125

*A Louisiana Swamp*
Charcoal and white chalk on paper
15⅜ x 19 inches
1989.01.116

*Near Yazoo Pass, Mississippi*
Oil on board, 17½ x 14 inches
1989.01.115

*West Bayou Plaquemines*
Oil on canvas, 12½ x 19 inches
1989.07.279

GARI MELCHERS
*Sketch of a Black Lady in a
White Dress and Hat*
Oil on paper, 18½ x 11 inches
1989.01.117

EMMA BELL MILES
*Tennessee Landscape*
Pastel on paper, 15 x 18 inches
1989.01.118

R. A. MILLER
*Creatures and Blow Oskar
with Pipe*
Magic marker on sheet metal
18 x 30 inches
1991.008

RICKY MILLER
*Lady Down the Street*
Pen-knife tableau, pine and
polychrome, 17 x 11 x 12 inches
1992.002

CLARENCE MILLET
*Louisiana Bayou*
Oil on board, 11½ x 15 inches
1989.05.261

*View of the Prudhomme-
Rouquier House, Natchitoches*
Oil on canvas, 31 x 36 inches
1992.029

CLARK MILLS
*Jackson Equestrian Statue*
Zinc alloy with bronze finish
23½ x 20 x 8½ inches
1989.03.236

NANCY THOMPSON MILLS
*Between Fine Arts and P.A.T.*
Oil on cardboard, 17 x 20 inches
1990.027

*Weekend By the Sea*
Oil on canvas, 60 x 48 inches
1990.093

GEORGE BERTRAND
MITCHELL
*Going to Market*
Pastel on paper, 16 x 20 inches
1989.01.119

ANDRES MOLINARY
*Landscape with Live Oak*
Oil on canvas, 16¾ x 26½ inches
1989.06.272

JOHN A. MOONEY
*Still Life - Flowers*
Oil on canvas, 12 x 18 inches
1989.01.121

*Surprise Attack near Harper's
Ferry, 1863*
Oil on canvas, 54⅛ x 96¼ inches
1989.01.120

BEULAH MOORE
*Basket of Grapes*
Oil on canvas, 11¼ x 16¼ inches
1989.01.122

ELEMORE MORGAN JR.
*New Field*
Acrylic on masonite, 42½ x 48 inches
1990.105

*Early Homesite*
Acrylic on masonite, 26 x 54¼ inches
1990.107

*Mid-Summer*
Acrylic on masonite, 16⅜ x 48 inches
1990.106

*Cows in Passing*
Acrylic on masonite, 41½ x 78 inches
1990.108

SISTER GERTRUDE MORGAN
*The New Jerusalem*
Ink and tempera on cardboard
3½ x 6 inches
1989.07.280

**HAL ALEXANDER COURTNEY MORRISON**
*Weighing the Cotton*
Oil on canvas, 31½ x 45½ inches
1989.01.123

**CHARLES W. MUNDAY**
*Tail Light*
Watercolor on, 20 x 28 inches
1991.015

**CHRISTOPHER A.D. MURPHY JR.**
*Barnard Street Slip*
Pencil and charcoal on paper
8½ x 11 inches
1989.01.137

*Green Kimono*
Oil on canvas, 22 x 18 inches
1989.01.134

*Joe Street, Savannah*
Charcoal on paper, 9¾ x 15½ inches
1989.01.136

*Theresa in Orange*
Oil on canvas, 20¼ x 24 inches
1989.01.135

**CHRISTOPHER PATRICK HUSSEY MURPHY**
*Big Top*
Watercolor on board
9¾ x 14¾ inches
1989.01.125

*Rosin Gang*
Pastel on board, 12¼ x 18½ inches
1989.01.124

*Still Life with Roses*
Watercolor, pencil on board
15¹⁄₁₆ x 10⅝ inches
1989.02.230

**LUCILE DESBOUILLONS MURPHY**
*Black Man Seated on a Chair*
Sepia wash on paper
12⅝ x 9¹⁄₁₆ inches
1989.01.126

*Still Life - Red, Pink and Yellow Roses in a Vase*
Watercolor on paper, 12 x 9 inches
1989.01.128

*Still Life - Vase of Nasturtiums*
Watercolor on paper, 12 x 9 inches
1989.01.127

**MARGARET A. MURPHY**
*Courtyard, Columbia University, New York City*
Oil on board, 19⅞ x 15¼ inches
1989.01.131

*Perry Lane and Bull Street, Savannah, Georgia*
Oil on canvas, 32 x 25 inches
1989.01.132

*Still Life - Green Foil and Red Chrysanthemums*
Oil on canvasboard, 20 x 16 inches
1989.01.130

*Still Life with Guitar*
Oil on canvas, 19¾ x 23¹⁵⁄₁₆ inches
1989.01.133

*Tybee Beach*
Oil on canvas-textured paper
20 x 15⅞ inches
1989.01.129

**FAITH C. MURRAY**
*Edisto Life*
Gouache on paper, 28 x 23 inches
1989.01.138

**GREGG MURRAY**
*Dropping In: Pintail Ducks*
Scratchboard, 16 x 23¼ inches
1989.09.289

*First Year*
Scratchboard, 13¼ x 19¼ inches
1990.030

**CHARLES FREDERICK NAEGELE**
*The Garden Path*
Oil on canvas, 25 x 21½ inches
1989.01.139

**JOHN NAEGLE**
*Portrait of Richard Mentor Johnson*
Oil on canvas
36¼ x 25¼ inches
1989.01.140

**ANNE TAYLOR NASH**
*Lady in a Porch Chair*
Oil on canvas, 34¾ x 30 inches
1989.01.141

*Nude - Reclining Female*
Oil on canvas, 34 x 45 inches
1989.01.142

*Reclining Lady*
Oil on canvas, 17 x 19 inches
1989.01.143

*Two Women*
Oil on canvas, 39⅞ x 39⅞ inches
1990.120

**ROBERT LOFTIN NEWMAN**
*Rabboni*
Oil on canvas, 16⅛ x 20⅛ inches
1989.01.144

**WILLIE BETTY NEWMAN**
*Still Life*
Oil on canvas, 19½ x 23½ inches
1989.01.145

**PAUL NINAS**
*Head of a Young Girl*
Charcoal on paper, 21⅝ x 17⅝ inches
1989.05.263

*Swamp Scene*
Watercolor on paper, 15¾ x 12 inches
1989.05.264

*Untitled abstract*
Oil on canvas, 47½ x 61 inches
1989.05.262

**THOMAS SATTERWHITE NOBLE**
*The Price of Blood*
Oil on canvas, 39¼ x 49½ inches
1989.03.237

**AUGUSTA OELSCHIG**
*Along the Tracks, Savannah*
Oil on board, 15⅛ x 37⅛ inches
1989.01.148

*Lynching*
Gouache on paper, 19½ x 24 inches
1989.01.149

*Play Ball*
Oil on canvas, 17 x 25 inches
1989.01.146

*Rhythm Diggers*
Oil on panel, 40 x 22 inches
1989.01.147

*Shouting*
Tempera on panel, 7½ x 19½ inches
1989.01.150

*Sunflowers*
Mixed media on board
38¼ x 28½ inches
1989.01.151

**JOHANNES ADAM SIMON OERTEL**
*South Carolina Marsh*
Oil on board, 18½ x 24½ inches
1989.01.152

**CLARA WEAVER PARRISH**
*Nude Model*
Oil on canvas, 18¼ x 14¼ inches
1989.01.153

**MARY FLOURNOY PASSAILAIGUE**
*At the Foot of Pine Mountain*
Oil on canvas, 23¾ x 29¾ inches
1990.041

*Carousel*
Watercolor on paper, 14½ x 21½ inches
1990.061

*Coming Shower, Sea Island*
Watercolor on paper, 14¾ x 23 inches
1990.048

*Cypress*
Watercolor on paper, 21 x 27 inches
1990.060

*Cypress Swamp*
Watercolor on paper, 14¾ x 11¼ inches
1990.059

*The End of the Season*
Watercolor on paper, 14 x 21 inches
1990.051

*Farmer's Market, Columbus*
Oil on canvas, 24 x 26 inches
1990.035

*Gray Skies, Sea Island*
Watercolor on paper, 22½ x 30 inches
1990.054

*The House on Hanover Square, Brunswick, Georgia*
Watercolor on paper, 21 x 29½ inches
1990.033

*Jekyll Island*
Watercolor on paper, 22 x 30½ inches
1990.057

*Mist o'er the Dunes, Sea Island*
Watercolor on paper, 15 x 22¾ inches
1990.049

*Mountain Country, North Georgia*
Oil on canvas, 16 x 20 inches
1990.039

*The Oaks at Cumberland Island*
Watercolor on paper, 22½ x 30½ inches
1990.055

*Okefenokee*
Oil on canvas, 16 x 12 inches
1990.046

*Rain and the Raspberry Roof, Columbus*
Oil on canvas, 16 x 24¼ inches
1990.042

*Reeves Store, Waverly Hall, Georgia*
Watercolor on paper, 15 x 22 inches
1990.047

*Reflections and Refractions*
Watercolor on paper, 14¼ x 21¼ inches
1990.052

*The Rickety Rackety Pier*
Watercolor on paper, 14½ x 20¼ inches
1990.034

*Road to the Marsh*
Oil on academy board
24¼ x 29⅞ inches
1990.040

*Still Life with Blue Glass*
Oil on canvas, 17½ x 21½ inches
1990.038

*Still Life with White Pitcher*
Oil on canvas, 20 x 24 inches
1990.043

*Summer Day, Sea Island*
Watercolor on paper, 22½ x 30 inches
1990.056

*Summer Flowers II*
Oil on canvas, 24 x 36 inches
1990.044

*Summer Skies*
Watercolor on paper, 20½ x 27¾ inches
1990.053

*Sun Flowers*
Oil on canvas, 20 x 16 inches
1990.037

*Three Girls*
Oil on canvas, 20 x 24 inches
1990.045

*Two Boats*
Oil on canvas, 12 x 18 inches
1990.036

*Untitled, Marsh Scene*
Watercolor on paper, 22 x 30½ inches
1990.058

*Untitled, Sea Island*
Watercolor on paper, 21¼ x 29½ inches
1990.050

**FRANCIS PAVY**
*Storm on the Coast*
Oil on canvas, 20 x 20 inches
1990.110

*Betting Money on the Cockfight*
Oil on canvas, 37 x 37 inches
1990.109

**ACHILLE PERELLI**
*Dead Game 1*
Watercolor, 16 x 9¾ inches
1989.06.274

*Turkey with Poult*
Oil on canvas, 26¼ x 19⅝ inches
1989.06.273

**ACHILLE PERETTI**
*Portrait of a Man*
Oil on canvas, 21½ x 17 inches
1989.07.281

**REV. B. F. PERKINS**
*Cherokee Love Birds*
Acrylic on wood, 48 x 29 inches
1992.013

*Doodle Bugs*
Acrylic on wood, 48 x 60 inches
1992.012

*10 Commandments to Live By*
House paint on wood, 24 x 36 inches
1992.015

*Gregorian vs. Julian Calendar*
Acrylic on canvas, 24½ x 34½ inches
1991.004

*My Epatha*
Acrylic on canvas, 24 x 36 inches
1992.014

**ENOCH WOOD PERRY**
*Good Doggie*
Oil on board, 15 x 12 inches
1989.01.154

**WILLIAM J. PETRIE**
*Dog Thief*
Acrylic on canvas, 24 x 20 inches
1990.016

*Occasional Chair*
Acrylic on canvas, 28 x 32 inches
1990.015

**HOBSON PITTMAN**
*August Afternoon*
Oil on canvas, 30 x 20 inches
1990.126

*Carnations II*
Oil on panel, 41½ x 29⅜ inches
1990.127

*Garden Party*
Oil on panel, 29½ x 41⅝ inches
1990.128

**LUCIEN WHITING POWELL**
*The Old Log Cabin*
Oil on canvas, 30 x 25 inches
1989.01.155

**MARGARET RAMSEY**
*Swing Low Sweet Chariot*
Oil on canvas, 16 x 20 inches
1990.066

*Georgia Pine Limb*
Oil on canvas, 24 x 36 inches
1990.022

*The Ice Cream Man*
Oil on canvas, 24 x 30 inches
1990.023

*Santa's Great Chimney*
Oil on canvas, 16 x 20 inches
1990.021

**JOHN W. RASER**
*Still Life in Landscape - Peaches and Grapes*
Oil on canvas, 12½ x 9⅝ inches
1989.01.156

**PAMELA HART VINTON BROWN RAVENEL**
*Southern Gothic*
Oil on canvas, 30 x 40 inches
1989.01.158

*Two Sisters - St. Mary's, Georgia*
Oil on canvas, 30 x 30 inches
1989.01.157

**POPEYE REED**
*Sandstone relief carving*
Sandstone, 12 x 16 inches
1990.123

**EDWARD RICE**
*Dormer*
Oil on canvas, 48 x 48 inches
1990.092

**JIM RICHARD**
*Squaring Off Downstairs*
Acrylic on canvas, 40 x 50 inches
1992.023

*Owning Modern Sculpture XXVI*
Acrylic on canvas, 55 x 4¼ inches
1992.028

**THOMAS ADDISON RICHARDS**
*Encountering an Alligator*
Oil on canvas, 21¼ x 30 inches
1989.01.159

*River Plantation*
Oil on canvas, 20¼ x 30 inches
1989.01.161

*Still Life - Basket of Peaches*
Oil on canvas, 14 x 12 inches
1989.01.160

**AIDEN LASSELL RIPLEY**
*Cabin in Georgia*
Watercolor on paper, 21 x 30 inches
1989.03.238

*Picnic*
Watercolor on paper, 21 x 28½ inches
1989.01.164

*Planters in a Field*
Watercolor on paper, 21⅛ x 30¼ inches
1989.01.163

*Unexpected Point, Florence, South Carolina*
Watercolor on Paper, 20 x 30⅝ inches
1989.01.162

**ROSETTA RAULSTON RIVERS**
*Cotton*
Oil on board, 18 x 24 inches
1989.01.165

**GEORGE RODRIGUE**
*The Cabin on the Beaudreaux Farm*
Oil on canvas, 16 x 20 inches
1990.017

**HARRY ROSELAND**
*The Co'tin*
Oil on canvas, 20 x 30 inches
1989.01.166

**JAMES MAHLON ROSEN**
*The Bull*
Oil/wax-oil emulsion on canvas
14 x 14 inches
1991.002

*The Birds of Pompeii*
Bound Sketchbook: ink and graphite on paper, 12 x 8½ x ½ inches
1991.014

**MARGARET ROSS**
*26th Street Tavern Blues Band*
Acrylic on canvasboard
11⅛ x 15½ inches
1990.077

*Sea World*
Acrylic on canvasboard
16 x 19¾ inches
1990.076

**ANDREE RUELLAN**
*Morning on the River*
Gouache on paper, 12¼ x 18½ inches
1989.01.167

**BETTY FOY SANDERS**
*Little Saint Simons Island*
Acrylic on canvas, 29¼ x 39¼ inches
1992.008

**HATTIE SAUSSY**
*In the Hall*
Oil on board, 20 x 24 inches
1989.01.168

*Myrtle Jones*
Oil on board, 20 x 16 inches
1989.01.169

*Portrait - Girl in Red*
Oil on board, 24 x 20 inches
1989.01.171

*Still Life - Vase of Zinnias*
Oil on Board, 15⅞ x 19¾ inches
1989.01.172

*Stream in Wooded Landscape*
Oil on canvasboard
15⅞ x 11⅞ inches
1989.01.170

**PAUL SAWYIER**
*Fishing Club, Jamaica Bay, New York*
Oil on academy board, 14 x 17 inches
1989.04.253

*Kentucky River Valley*
Oil on canvas 14 x 17 inches
1989.04.254

**WILLIAM HARRISON SCARBOROUGH**
*Portrait of Young Girl and Man*
Oil on canvas, 49¾ x 39½ inches
1989.01.173

**SCHOOL OF HOWARD CHANDLER CHRISTIE**
*Confederate Honor Roll*
Oil on linen, 18 x 60 inches
1989.07.282

**CHARLES SHANNON**
*Saturday Night*
Oil on canvas, 34 x 24 inches
1989.01.174

**FRANK SHAPLEIGH**
*In Charlotte Street - St. Augustine, Florida, 1891*
Oil on canvas, 10 x 15⅞ inches
1989.01.175

**JAMES HAMILTON SHEGOGUE**
*Colored Slave*
Oil on panel, 8 x 6¹⁵⁄₁₆ inches
1989.01.176

**NELL CHOATE SHUTE**
*All Over But the Shoutin, 1942*
Watercolor on paper, 14 x 21 inches
1989.01.177

*Apple for Teacher*
Pastel on paper, 23¾ x 17¾ inches
1989.01.181

*Coal Dump, Atlanta*
Watercolor on paper, 21¼ x 29¼ inches
1989.01.178

*Passing Time*
Oil on canvas, 14¼ x 24 inches
1989.01.182

*Taking up the Peachtree Tracks*
Watercolor on paper, 15 x 22 inches
1989.01.183

*Walter Hill Fishing*
Watercolor on paper, 19½ x 25½ inches
1989.01.180

*Water Tower, Atlanta*
Watercolor on paper, 22 x 30 inches
1989.01.179

**WILLIAM POSEY SILVA**
*Chattanooga from Lookout Mountain*
Oil on board, 8⅞ x 11¾ inches
1989.01.184

*Fisherman's Hut on the Ashley, 1944*
Oil on board, 20 x 24 inches
1989.02.233

*Raiment of Springtime*
Oil on canvas, 10⅛ x 24 inches
1989.01.185

**DAVID SILVETTE**
*Uncle Josh*
Oil on canvas, 51⅛ x 38¼ inches
1989.01.186

**ALICE RAVENEL HUGER SMITH**
*Bayou Scene*
Watercolor on Whatman board
21½ x 16¾ inches
1989.01.188

*Golden Stalks and Egrets*
Watercolor on Whatman board
21½ x 16¾ inches
1989.01.187

*Waterway in Spring*
Watercolor on paper, 12½ x 6½ inches
1989.01.189

**MARY T. SMITH**
*Red Figure on Blue*
House paint on corrugated tin
52¼ x 26⅞ inches
1990.134

**WILLIAM THOMPSON RUSSELL SMITH**
*Baptism in Virginia*
Oil on canvas, 19¼ x 28¼ inches
1989.01.192

*Mount Vernon*
Oil on canvas, 12 x 18 inches
1989.01.191

*View of Charlottesville*
Watercolor on paper, 11 x 16¼ inches
1989.01.190

**XANTHUS SMITH**
*Battle of the Kearsarge and Alabama*
Watercolor on board, 19¾ x 29¾ inches
1989.01.193

*Landscape with Boats*
Oil on canvas, 15¼ x 23½ inches
1992.027

**SOTHERLAND**
*Portrait of Clementine Hunter*
Oil on board, 30 x 22 inches
1989.07.283

**MARION SOUCHON**
*Maison Maurice*
Oil on board, 28 x 22 inches
1990.111

**NINA HOWELL STARR**
*Gift to Minnie Evans from George Rountree, Jr.*
Black and white photograph
8 x 10 inches
1990.012

*Minnie Evans and George Rountree Jr. at Airlie Gate*
Color photograph
14 x 11 inches
1990.010

*Minnie Evans at Airlie Gatehouse*
Black and white photograph
8 x 10 inches
1990.011

*Minnie Evans in New York 1973*
Black and white photograph
8 x 10 inches
1990.013

**WILL HENRY STEVENS**
*Abstraction*
Watercolor on paper, 16 x 14 inches
1989.01.194

*The Brook*
Charcoal on paper, 17 x 14 inches
1989.01.196

*Still Life -Flowers with Distant Mountains*
Oil on canvas, 36½ x 30½ inches
1990.121

*Musical Abstraction*
Watercolor on paper, 19⅞ x 13⅞ inches
1989.01.195

**CLARA BARRETT STRAIT**
*Tabletop Still Life - Rhododendron in Black Vase*
Oil on board, 30 x 20 inches
1989.01.197

**MEYER STRAUS**
*Bayou Teche*
Oil on canvas, 30 x 60 inches
1989.03.239

**CARRIE STUBBS**
*Charleston Bride*
Oil on canvas, 36 x 25⅞ inches
1989.01.198

**JIMMY LEE SUDDUTH**
*Log Cabin*
Sugared paint on wood
15¾ x 17¼ inches
1990.075

*Football Players*
Acrylic on display board
16 x 22⅞ inches
1990.130

*Self Portrait*
Tempera on plywood, 48 x 24 inches
1991.005

**GEORGE WASHINGTON SULLY**
*Episcopal Church, Appalachicola, Florida*
Watercolor on paper, 4¼ x 6¼ inches
1989.01.199

*The House We Lived In*
Watercolor on paper, 3⅜ x 5 inches
1989.02.232

*New Orleans Rack Picture*
Watercolor on paper, 6½ x 8 inches
1989.01.200

*View of Episcopal Church*
Watercolor on paper, 6⅜ x 7½ inches
1989.02.231

**HENRY OSSAWA TANNER**
*Georgia Landscape*
Oil on canvas, 17¼ x 32¼ inches
1989.01.201

**ANNA HEYWARD TAYLOR**
*Low Country Azalea*
Watercolor on paper
21¾ x 13¾ inches
1989.10.290

*Swamp Azaleas*
Watercolor on paper, 22 x 16 inches
1989.01.203

*Swamp Azaleas 1929*
Watercolor on paper, 20 x 14 inches
1989.01.202

*White Herons*
Watercolor on paper, 22½ x 15⅝ inches
1989.01.204

**ANTHONY THIEME**
*Charleston Doorway*
Oil on canvas, 30½ x 36½ inches
1989.01.205

**ALFRED WORDSWORTH THOMPSON**
*Watching for the Train*
Oil on canvas, 14 x 20 inches
1992.035

**EUGENE A. THOMPSON**
*Christ Preaching on the Mount, Eve of the Great Feast, A.D.33*
Ink, pencil and scratchboard technique on gessoed panel
38½ x 48 inches
1989.01.206

**THURE DE THULSTRUP (BROR THURE THULSTRUP)**
*Battle of Shiloh - The Hornet's Nest*
Watercolor and pencil on paper
17¼ x 24¾ inches
1989.01.208

*Sketch of Battle of Kennesaw Mountain*
Pencil, ink, ink wash and white gouache on paper
16¾ x 23⅜ inches
1989.01.207

**MOSE TOLLIVER**
*Black Crucifix with Birds*
Enamel on plywood, 48 x 19¾ inches
1990.133

*Bird Tree*
Tempera on masonite
32½ x 14¾ inches
1990.081

**JOHN MARTIN TRACY**
*A Field Trial - A Shot*
Oil on canvas, 30 x 50 inches
1989.03.241

**OLIN TRAVIS**
*Cabin in the Ozarks*
Oil on canvas, 35 x 47 inches
1989.01.209

**BILL TRAYLOR**
*Figures and Construction*
Construction color and gouache on board, 10⅝ x 7¼ inches
1989.01.210

**HELEN TURNER**
*A Country Road*
Pencil on paper, 10⅞ x 17 inches
1989.05.266

**UNKNOWN**
*Constitution window shade*
Oil on silk, mounted on canvas
36 x 26 inches
1989.01.008

*The Lost Cause ("M")*
Oil on canvas, 19¾ x 26¹³⁄₁₆ inches
1989.01.004

*Monitor Engaging a Sailing Vessel*
Oil on ticking, 12¼ x 17½ inches
1989.01.007

*Moses in the Bullrushes*
Oil and crewel on muslin
29½ x 60 inches
1989.01.003

*Portrait of a Lady in a Landscape*
Oil on board, 48 x 34 inches
1989.01.098

*Portrait of Alton Pemberton, Jr.*
Oil on board, 15⅝ x 12½ inches
1989.01.006

*Portrait of Rebecca Brown*
Oil on canvas, 26¼ x 26¼ inches
1989.01.002

*Secessionville, South Carolina, from Black Island*
Watercolor and pencil on paper
5⅝ x 8¹¹⁄₁₆ inches
1989.01.005

*Natural Bridge of Virginia*
Oil on canvas, 25½ x 33¾ inches
1990.122

**ELIZABETH O'NEILL VERNER**
*Annie*
Pastel on silk, 17¼ x 13¼ inches
1989.01.212

*The Flower Vendor*
Pastel on silk, 27⅞ x 23 inches
1989.01.211

*Sara*
Pastel on board, 17¼ x 13⅛ inches
1989.01.213

**GEORGE LEWIS VIAVANT**
*Birds*
Watercolor on paper, 16⅝ x 10⅜ inches
1989.05.267

*Meadowlark*
Watercolor on paper, 16⅝ x 10¼ inches
1989.01.214

**FERDINAND GRAHAM WALKER**
*My Old Kentucky Home*
Oil on board, 12 x 18 inches
1989.01.215

**WILLIAM AIKEN WALKER**
*At the Levee*
Oil on panel, 6¼ x 12⅛ inches
1989.03.246

*Boy with Goat*
Oil on board, 11 x 8 inches
1989.03.248

*Cabin Scene*
Watercolor on paper, 6⅛ x 8⅞ inches
1989.01.217

*The Cotton Pickers*
Oil on artist's palette, 7¼ x 5 inches
1989.03.245

*Cotton Picking*
Oil on board, 6 x 12 inches
1989.07.284

*In the Cottonfields*
Oil on canvas, 20 x 12 inches
1989.03.242

*Man with Basket of Cotton*
Oil on board, 13½ x 6½ inches
1990.018

*Old Man in a Cottonfield*
Oil on board, 11⅞ x 7⅝ inches
1989.03.244

*Opossum Hunting*
Pencil on paper, 6½ x 8⅜ inches
1989.01.216

*Pair of Charleston Market Vendors*
Oil on board, pair: 8 x 3¹⁄₁₆ inches
1989.03.243

*Plantation Portrait*
Oil on canvas, 14 x 24 inches
1989.03.247

*The Road to Rosalie*
Oil on board, 10¼ x 18 inches
1989.03.240

*Roustabout on Wharf*
Oil on board, 12 x 6 inches
1990.085

**ANDREW JOHN HENRY WAY**
*An Abundance of Fruit*
Oil on canvas, 22 x 30 inches
1989.08.288

*Self-portrait*
Oil on ivory, 2⁹⁄₁₆ x 2⁵⁄₁₆ inches
1989.03.249

**HOWARD (MARIA HOWARD) WEEDEN**
*Violinist*
Watercolor on paperboard
9 x 6⅞ inches
1989.01.220

*You'll Remember Me*
Watercolor on paper, 9 x 6⅞ inches
1989.01.219

*Young Woman in Blue*
Watercolor on paperboard
9 x 6⅞ inches
1989.01.218

H.T. WEST
*Sharecroppers*
Pen and ink on paper
12⅛ x 16¼ inches
1989.01.221

WILLIAM EDWARD WEST
*Portrait of William Rufus Gray Bates*
Oil on canvas, 12⅝ x 10⅝ inches
1989.01.222

ELIZABETH WHITE
*Woodland Idyll, Brookgreen Gardens*
Pastel on paper, 16½ x 11½ inches
1989.01.223

*River Landscape - Summer*
Watercolor on paper, 9½ x 13½ inches
1989.01.224

MABLE DUNN WHITE
*Charleston Shrimp Boats, 1941*
Watercolor on paper, 14 x 22 inches
1989.01.225

WADE WHITE
*Ravenel & Rivers, Charleston, South Carolina*
Oil on canvas, 29½ x 38 inches
1990.091

WILLIE WHITE
*Planet with Eagles and Dinosaur*
Marker on illustration board
22 x 28 inches
1990.135

THOMAS WIGHTMAN
*Strawberries*
Oil on canvas, 9 x 16 inches
1989.01.226

FRANK NELSON WILCOX
*Lowland Cabin*
Watercolor on paper, 18½ x 29¼ inches
1989.01.227

CATHERINE WILEY
*Tennessee Landscape*
Oil on canvas, 18 x 12 inches
1990.068

ELEANOR MCADOO WILEY
*Tennessee Farm Building*
Oil on canvas, 16¼ x 13 inches
1990.070

*Winter Grisaille*
Oil on canvas, 18¾ x 12⅛ inches
1990.071

*Old Wiley Homestead, Lake City, Tenn.*
Oil on canvas, 15½ x 20⅛ inches
1990.072

*Portrait of Catherine Wiley*
Oil on canvas, 16¼ x 12¼ inches
1990.069

EMMA CHEVES WILKINS
*Blue Jug and Camellias*
Oil on canvas, 23 x 21 inches
1989.01.228

*Red Azaleas, Bonaventure Cemetery, Savannah*
Oil on board, 14 x 16 inches
1989.01.229

ROBERT B. WILSON
*Lions*
Watercolor on paper, 14½ x 21 inches
1990.019

GEORGE WOLTZE (attr.)
*The Sunny South*
Oil on canvas, 28 x 39 inches
1990.124

ELLSWORTH WOODWARD
*Portrait of Joseph Meyer*
Oil on linen, 20 x 16 inches
1989.05.268

*Portrait of Tony*
Oil on linen, 18 x 15 inches
1989.05.269

WILLIAM WOODWARD
*Seashore Scene*
Oil on canvas, 13¼ x 17⅜ inches
1989.05.27

*Summer Home - Biloxi or "Hopkins Looking In"*
Oil on artist board, 12⅝ x 19⅜ inches
1989.07.285

*View Toward Old Bain Street*
Oil on canvas, 14¾ x 19 inches
1989.05.271

***Jacket/Cover Illustration***, A.J.H. WAY, An Abundance of Fruit

## *Chapter Illustrations*

Antebellum Portraiture, (20-21), NICOLA MARSHALL, *Young Girl with Cat*
Art of the Civil War, (32-33), JOHN A. MOONEY, *Surprise Attack Near Harper's Ferry.*
The Black Presence in Southern Painting, (44-45), ELEANORA GIBSON HOUSTON, *First Communion*
Southern Still-Life Art, (56-57), ELLA SOPHONISBA HERGESHEIMER, *Gladiolas in a Blue Vase*
Landscape Painting in the South, (68-69), MEYER STRAUS, *Bayou Teche*
Southern Impressionism, (94-95), GEORGE WOLTZ, *The Sunny South*
Works on Paper (122-123), ALEXANDER JOHN DRYSDALE, *Bayou Landscape*
Twentieth-Century Art, (144-145), HOBSON PITTMAN, *Garden Party*
The Self-Taught Southern Artist, (178-179), MINNIE EVANS, *Ark of the Covenant*
Contemporary Southern Painting, (210-211), DON COOPER, *Extreme Southeast Georgia*

# Index

**A**

Abbot, John - 124, 125, 237
*Abstraction* (Ninas) - 160, 161
*Abundance of Fruit, An* (Way) - 60, 61
Adams, Wayman - 45, 50, 51, 138, 237
*Aeon-Angel-Metempsychosis* (Jennings) - 204, 205
Alferez, Enrique - 237
Alke, Stephen - 237
"America As Art" exhibition - 14
"American Painters of the South" exhibition - 11
Anderson, Walter Inglis - 142, 143, 237
Antebellum Portraiture - 20-30
*Apollo and the Muses* (Barnard) -126,127
*Ark of the Covenant* (Evans) - 178,179, 182, 183
Armstrong, Zebedee Jr. - 188-189, 237
"Art and Artists of the South" exhibition - 9, 10, 17, 18, 33
Audubon, John James - 237
Avent, Mayna Treanor - 237

**B**

Backus, A.E. - 237
*Bargain Basement* (Dodd) - 162, 163
Barnard, Mr. - 126, 127
*Basket of Peaches* (Richards) - 58, 59
Bates, David - 222, 223, 237
*Battle of Kearsarge and Alabama* (Smith) - 40, 41
*Bayou Landscape* (Drysdale) - 132, 133
*Bayou Landscape* (Meeker) - 84, 85
*Bayou Teche* (Straus) - 68, 69, 74, 75
*Beech Trees* (Brenner) - 80, 81
Belcher, Hilda - 237
Bell, Bessie - 237
Bell, Wenona Day - 237
Berchmans, Sister Agnes - 237
*Betting Money on the Cockfight* (Pavy) - 232, 233
Betts, Louis L. - 110, 111, 237
*Black Crucifix with Birds* (Tolliver) - 196, 197
*Black Jesus* (Hunter) - 184, 185
Black Presence in Southern Art - 44-55
Blair, Jeanette Kenney - 237
*Blue Parrots, Florida* (Hull) - 146, 147
*Blowing Trees* (Brewer) - 180, 181
Boisset, Charles L. - 237
Bourgeois, Douglas - 222, 226, 227, 237
*Box with Cups, Year of 1986* (Armstrong) - 188-189
Brenner, Carl Christian - 80, 81, 90, 237
Brewer, Ralph - 180, 181, 237
Brook, Alexander - 237
Brown, Roger - 228, 229, 237
Burchfield, Charles Ephraim - 237

Busby, Buzz - 237
Burnside, Richard - 190, 191

**C**

Cabaniss, Lila - 112
Carr, Lyell - 237
Carson, Caroline - 237,238
Chambers, Willie M. - 238
Chapman, Conrad Wise - 33, 36
*Charleston Bride* (Stubbs) - 54, 55
*Charleston Doorway* (Thieme) - 120, 121
*Cherokee Love Birds* (Perkins) - 206, 207
Christie, Howard Chandler, School of - 242
Civil War, art of 32-43
Clark, Eliot Candee - 106, 107, 238
Cleaveland, John - 238
Coles, Ann Cadwallader - 238
*Constitution Window Shade* (Artist Unknown) - 243
Cook, August - 238
Cook, Irma - 238
Cooper, Don - 210,211, 222, 230, 231, 238
Coggins Collection - 18, 76
Coggins, Dr. Robert Powell - 6, 17, 18
Contemporary Southern Art - 210-235
Coulon, George David - 88, 89, 238
*Country Road, A* (Turner) - 128, 129
Craig, Elizabeth E. - 238
Crawford, Josephine M. - 238
*Cubist Mountain View* (Stevens) - 140, 141

**D**

Daingerfield, Elliott - 92, 93, 238
*Defending a Battery - Confederate Cavalry Charge* (Forbes) - 34, 35
Dodd, Lamar - 162, 163, 172, 238
Dodge, William de Leftwich - 238
*Dog Thief* (Petrie) - 224, 225
*Dormer* (Rice) - 216, 217, 238
Drysdale, Alexander John - 69, 80, 122, 123, 132, 133, 180, 238
Dubreuil, Victor - 238
Dureau, George - 220, 221

**E**

*Early Homesite* (Morgan) - 218, 219
Evans, Minnie - 118,119,182,183, 238
*Extreme Southeast Georgia* (Cooper) - 210, 211, 230, 231
*Eye Have the Hand that Holds the Staff for the Ancestors' Sake* (Holley) -198,199

**F**

*Fall Pin Oaks with Birds* (Anderson) - 142, 143

Faulkner, Henry - 176, 177, 238
*Field Trial - A Shot* (Tracy) - 82, 83
Finster, Howard - 202, 203, 238
*First Communion* (Houston) - 44,45, 52, 53
Forbes, Edwin Austin - 34, 35, 238
Foster, E.T.H. - 78, 79, 238
Fowler, Trevor Thomas - 24, 25, 238
Fraser, Charles - 238
Frerichs, William Charles Anthony - 30, 31, 70, 71, 78, 238

**G**

*Garden Party* (Pittman) - 144,145, 174, 175
Gasser, Henry - 239
Gaul, William Gilbert - 42, 43, 238
*Georgia Landscape* (Tanner) - 86, 87
*Georgia Red Clay* (Jones) - 168, 169
*Gladiolas in a Blue Vase* (Hergesheimer) - 56, 57, 66, 67
Goekjian, Karekin - 239
Golding, William - 239
Goldthwaite, Anne - 239
Gordon, Emeline H. - 239
Gordy, Robert - 212, 213, 239
Gregory, Angela - 239
Guerin, Rene - 239
Guignard, Caroline - 239
Gwathmey, Robert - 166, 167, 239

**H**

Hale, Ellen Day - 239
Harrington, W.H. - 239
Hartley, Rachel - 239
Hay, T.A. - 239
Heldner, Knute - 239
Hergesheimer, Ella Sophonisba - 15, 56, 57, 66, 67, 239
Herndon, Willina S. - 24
Herzog, Herman - 239
Heustis, Louise - 239
Higgins, George F. - 76, 77, 239
Hoehn, Nancy - 239
Holley, Lonnie - 198, 199, 239
Houston, Eleanora Gibson - 44, 45, 52, 53, 239
Hudson, Walter Tiree - 239
Hull, Marie - 146, 147, , 239
Hunter, Clementine - 184, 185, 196, 239
*Hurricane Hugo* (Brown) - 228, 229
Hutty, Alfred - 136, 137, 138, 239

**I**

*I Can't Sleep* (McCrady) - 170, 171
*Ice Cream Man, The* (Ramsey) - 186, 187
Impressionism, Southern - 95-121

*In the Hall* (Saussy) - 112, 113
*Infantryman, the* (Gaul) - 42, 43
Inglesby, Helen Hatch - 239
Inness, George Jr. - 7, 239
Irvine, Sarah - 239
Irving, John Beaufain - 239
*Italian Caprice* (Coulon) - 87, 88

**J**

Jackson, Joseph - 239
Jarvis, John Wesley - 22, 23
Jennings, James Harold - 204, 205, 239
Joiner, Harvey - 80, 90, 91, 239
Jones, Myrtle - 239
Jones, Nell Choate - 168, 169, 239, 240
Joy, Sue - 239

**K**

Kempton, Susan - 240
*Kentucky River Valley* (Sawyier) - 102, 103
Kinney, Charles - 194, 195, 240
Kinsey, Alberta - 240
Kohlmeyer, Ida - 214, 215, 240

**L**

Lake Toxaway, North Carolina - 70
Lambdin, George Cochran - 62, 63, 240
Lambdin, James Reid - 62
Lambdin, Samuel - 62
Lambeth, Randy - 240
Lampkin, Melinda Moore - 240
Landscape Painting in the South - 69 -93
Lee, George D. - 240
Lemm, Adele - 240
Leydendecker, Joseph Christian - 240
Light, Joe E. - 240
Lloyd, Frank B. - 240
London, Frank - 158, 159, 240
*Long Time Ago, A* (Turner) - 104, 105
*Lost Cause, The* ("Monogrammist M") - 38, 39, 243
*Lowland Landscape with Deer* (Mignot) - 72, 73
*Lowland Waterway by the Moonlight* (Smith) - 130, 131
Lucas, Charlie - 240
Lyle, James P. - 240

**M**

MacNeil, Hermon Atkins - 240
*Maison Maurice* (Souchon) - 164, 165
Malone, Blondelle - 240
Manning, Zelle - 240
Marschall, Nicola - 20, 21, 28, 29, 33, 240

Massey, Willie - 240
May, Florence Lister Land - 240
Mazzonovich, Lawrence - 240
McCord, J.T. (Jake) - 200, 201, 240
McCrady, John - 45, 170, 171, 240
McGehee, Alice - 240
McKenzie, Carl - 240
McLaws, Virginia Randall - 100, 101, 240
Meeker, Joseph Rusling - 33, 69, 80, 84, 85, 222, 240
Melchers, Gari - 134, 135, 240
Mignot, Louis Remy - 72, 73
Miles, Emma Bell - 240
Miller, R.A. - 240
Miller, Ricky - 240
Millet, Clarence - 118, 119, 240
Mills, Clark - 240
Mills, Nancy Thompson - 240
Mitchell, George Bertrand - 240
Moise, Theodore Sidney - 24
Molinary, Andres - 64, 104, 128, 240
*Mona Lisa* (Finster) - 202, 203
*Monitor Engaging a Sailing Vessel* (Artist Unknown) - 243
"Monogrammist M" - 38, 39
Mooney, John A. - 32, 33, 36, 37, 240
Moore, Beulah - 240
Morgan, Elemore Jr. - 218, 219, 240
Morgan, Sister Gertrude - 240
Morris Museum of Art - 6, 18, 19
Morrison, Alexander Courtney - 57, 64, 65, 241
*Moses in the Bullrushes* (Artist Unknown) - 243
Mosler, Henry - 38
*Mount Vernon* (Smith) - 8
*Mullet and Shells* (Bates) - 222, 223
Munday, Charles W. - 241
Murphy, Christopher A.D., Jr. - 19, 241
Murphy, Christopher P.H. - 241
Murphy, Lucille Desbouillons - 241
Murphy, Margaret A. - 241
Murray, Faith - 241
Murray, Gregg - 241
*Mythic Series # 5* (Kohlmeyer) - 214, 215

**N**
Naegele, Charles Frederick - 241
Naegle, John - 241
Nash, Anne Taylor - 150, 151, 241
*Natural Bridge of Virginia* (Artist Unknown) - 243
*New Orleans Mammy* (Adams) - 50, 51
Newman, Robert Loftin - 241
Newman, Willie Betty - 241
Ninas, Paul - 160, 161, 241
Noble, Thomas Satterwhite - 46, 47, 241

**O**
Oelschig, Augusta - 172, 173, 241
Oertel, Johannes Adam Simon - 241
*Owning Modern Sculpture XXVI* (Richard) - 234, 235

**P**
"Painting in the South" exhibition - 11, 16, 17
*Pale Yellow Throat* (Abbot) - 124, 125
Palfrey, family - 22
*Palm Grove, Florida* (Higgins) - 76, 77
Parrish, Clara - 241
Passailaigue, Mary - 241
Pavy, Francis - 232, 233, 241
Peale, Charles Wilson - 66
Perelli, Achille - 64, 241
Peretti, Achille - 241
Perkins, Benjamin F. - 206, 207, 242
Perry, Enoch Wood - 242
Petrie, William J. - 224, 225, 242
*Pahro of Egipt* (Burnside) - 190,191
Pittman, Hobson - 144, 145, 164, 174, 175, 242
*Plantation Portrait* (Walker) - 48, 49
*Play Ball* (Oelschig) - 172, 173
*Portrait of a Lady in a Landscape* (Artist Unknown) - 243
*Portrait of Alton Pemberton Jr.* (Artist Unknown) - 243
*Portrait of a Young Girl and Older Man* (Scarborough) - 26, 27
*Portrait of Mrs. William Palfrey* (Jarvis) - 22, 23
*Portrait of Rebecca Brown* (Artist Unknown) - 243
*Portrait of Tony* (Woodward) - 98, 99
Powell, Lucien Whiting - 242
*Price of Blood, The* (Noble) - 46, 47
*Prudhomme-Rouquier House, Natchitoches* (Millet) - 118, 119

**R**
*Raiment of Springtime* (Silva) - 116, 117
*Rainbow in Georgia* (Inness) - 7
Ramsey, Margaret - 186, 187, 242
Raser, John W. - 242
*Ravenel & Rivers Street* (White) 148, 149
Ravenel, Pamela Hart Vinton Brown - 152, 153, 242
Reed, Popeye - 242
*Red Figure on Blue* (Smith) - 192, 193
*Rehearsal in Ring Number 1* (Dureau) - 220, 221
*Reflections* (Gwathmey) - 166, 167
Rice, Edward - 216, 217, 242
Richard, Jim - 234, 235, 242
Richards, T. Addison - 57, 58, 59, 69, 242
Ripley, Aiden Lassell - 242
Rivers, Rosetta Raulston - 242
Robinson, Mrs. James F. - 24, 25
Rodrigue, George - 242
Roseland, Harry - 242
Rosen, James Mahlon - 242
*Roses* (Lambdin) - 62, 63
*Roses and Fuchsia* (Lambdin) - 62, 63
Ross, Margaret - 242
Ruellan, Andree - 242

**S**
Sanders, Betty Foy - 242
*Saturday Evening* (Shannon) - 154, 155

Saussy, Hattie - 112, 113, 242
*Savannah Harbor* (Clark) - 106, 107
Sawyier, Paul - 102, 103, 242
Scarborough, William Harrison - 26, 27, 242
*Scylla and Charybdis Factor, The* (Gordy) - 212, 213
*Secessionville, South Carolina . . .* (Artist Unknown) - 243
*Self Portrait* (Sudduth) - 208, 209
*Self Portrait at Easel* (McLaws) - 100, 101
Self-taught artists - 18, 19, 178-209
Shannon, Charles - 152, 172
Shapleigh, Frank - 242
Shegogue, James Hamilton - 242
Shute, Nell Choate - 242
Silva, William Posey - 116, 117, 242
*Sketch of Young Black Woman in White Dress* (Melchers) - 134, 135
Smith, Alice Ravenel Huger - 130 , 131, 242
Smith, Mary Tillman - 192, 193, 242
Smith, William Thompson Russell - 8, 40, 242
Smith, Xanthus - 40, 41, 243
Sotherland - 243
Souchon, Marion Sims - 164, 165, 243
*Southern Gothic* (Ravenel) - 152, 153
*Southern Mountain Landscape, North Carolina* (Frerichs) - 70, 71
Starr, Nina Howell - 243
Still-Life Art, Southern - 56-67
*Still Life: Flowers with Distant Mountains* (Stevens) - 156, 157
*Still Life with Golden Slipper* (Faulkner) - 176, 177
Stevens, Will Henry - 140, 141, 156, 157, 243
Strait, Clara Barrett - 243
Straus, Meyer - 74, 75, 243
Stubbs, Carrie - 54, 55, 243
Sudduth, Jimmy Lee - 208, 209, 243
*Suitcase, The* (Bourgeois) - 226, 227
Sully, George Washington - 243
Sully, Thomas - 12, 26
*Sunny South, The* (Woltze) - 94-97
*Sunset Glory* (Daingerfield) - 92, 93
*Surprise Attack Near Harper's Ferry* (Mooney) - 32, 33, 36, 37

**T**
Tanner, Henry Ossawa - 86, 87, 243
Taylor, Anna Heyward - 243
*Tennessee Landscape* (Wiley) - 108, 109
Thieme, Anthony - 120, 121, 243
Thompson, Alfred Wordsworth - 243
Thompson, Eugene A. - 243
Thulstrup, Bror Thure - 243
Tolliver, Mose - 196, 197, 243
Tracy, John Martin - 82, 83, 243
Travis, Olin - 243
Traylor, Bill - 243
*Trout* (Morrison) - 64, 65
Turner, Helen - 100, 104, 105, 128, 129, 146, 243
Twentieth-Century Art - 144-177
*Two Women* (Nash) - 150, 151
*Tyranny of Survival* (London) - 158, 159

**V**
Verner, Elizabeth O'Neill - 243
Viavant, George Lewis - 243
*Vase of Flowers, Drapery, Inkwell* (Hergesheimer) - 15
*View Toward Old Bain Street* (Woodward) - 114, 115

**W**
Walker, Ferdinand Graham - 243
Walker, William Aiken - 33, 45, 48, 49, 64, 243
Way, Andrew John Henry - 60, 61, 243
*We Saw 7 Rainbows 7 Suns This Day* (Kinney) - 194, 195
Weeden, (Maria) Howard - 243, 244
West, H.T. - 244
West, William Edward, 244
White, Elizabeth - 138, 139, 244
White, Mable Dunn - 244
White, Wade - 148, 149, 244
White, Willie - 244
*Wier, Lizzie Neigh* (Frerichs) - 30, 31
Wightman, Thomas - 244
Wilcox, Frank Nelson - 244
Wiley, Catherine - 100, 108, 109, 146, 244
WIley, Eleanor McAdoo - 244
Wilkins, Emma Cheves - 112, 172, 244
Wilson, Robert B. - 244
*Winged Alligator* (McCord) - 200, 201
Woltze, George - 94-97, 244
*Wooded Landscape* (Joiner) - 90, 91
*Woodland Idyll, Brookgreen Gardens* (White) - 138, 139
Woodward, Ellsworth - 98, 99, 244
Woodward, William - 98, 114, 115, 244
Works on Paper - 123-143
*Writing It Up - Heroic Soldier of the Pen* (Forbes) - 34, 35

**Y**
*Yellow Parasol, The* (Betts) - 110, 111
*Young Girl with Cat* (Marschall) - 20, 21, 28, 29

*A Southern Collection* was designed and electronically composed by Lydia M. Inglett for the opening of the Morris Museum of Art. The text is set in Fairfield, a slightly decorative typeface with old-style touches designed by Rudolph Ruzicka over 50 years ago for Linotype-Hell. 175-line color separations were produced by David Kaminsky of Savannah Color Separators.

This book was printed and bound using 100 lb. Sterling Gloss text by Horowitz/Rae Book Manufacturers of New Jersey.

*In life beauty perishes, but not in art.*